D1304401

Come visit my website for practical ideas, resource materials, and information about our workshops

www.nhie.net

To schedule future workshops, keynote addresses, or program evaluations, please call New Horizons In Education Inc.

(916) 482-4405
info@nhie.net

We look forward to your call!

Assessment - all about understanding one's story

  7 sec. to make 1st impression

  Lau vs Nichols - 1974 : Must provide equal access to core curriculum

  Biliteracy

  Endorsement (ESL)

p.2

INSPIRATION - comes from Latin
  - means to breathe from within

Practical
Brain-based
Ideas.

Contextualize the concept. Teach
concept through stories.

1. Foundation
  Frameworks   Good teaching is good teaching. Platitude that says "One size
  Tools   fits all." Not so.

Pattern books - The brain ~~seeks~~ is a patterns-seeking device.
  (esp. primary grades)
    "Bathe" students in language's rhythmic structure.

2. L^2 proficiency tests level always leads the parade

3. 4 B's

    Origins of RTI - meant to be used
        only w/ SPED.

Bilingual - beginner knows 5OO words
        at listening level

Woodcock Muños
  & LAS for
  placement

ELDA to monitor
  growth

p. 11

4. Transfer theory - huge tool for biliteracy
        You only learn to read once in your
        lifetime.

Founda- L^1 L^2 Bilin~~gual~~terate) in listening?
tion   speaking? - know how to change syntax
what do   writing?
we know   reading?
about 1st
language?

1st form of writing:
                drawing
  2nd : copying

1. Who makes decision to transition kids "out"?

2. On what is the decision based?

TABLE OF CONTENTS

BRAIN-BASED TOOLS: VOCABULARY DEVELOPMENT,

BRAIN-BASED TOOLS: COMPREHENSION

> ## "Everything in the classroom revolves around <u>relationships</u>.
> ## Take the time to understand all of the relationships."
>
> *Jo Gusman*

List 5 relationships we must be mindful of when teaching bilingual students how to read in English.

1.

2.

3.

4.

5.

FOUNDATION-FRAMEWORKS-TOOLS MODEL™

The 3 Building Blocks Needed To Create a Successful Language and Literacy Program For Your English Language Learners

Jo Gusman

FOUNDATION

How well do you know and understand your new clientele?

What do you believe about language? + −

i subtractive
additive
language acquisition

FRAMEWORKS

What theoretical frameworks do you use to make your curriculum and instruction decisions?

ELD comes _first_, then ELA (Listening & speaking first)

the research base for the frameworks you use second language acquisition, literacy, and bicognition?

TOOLS

What are the most effective strategies, processes, and skill development tech___ English Language Lea___

89% of all communication is not what you says, but how you say it.

ELLs need a
1. context.

2. prior knowledge hook check

Your English Language Learners Come To You With The 4 Bs

Jo Gusman

We need to ask "What do our English Language Learners know, instead of what do they not know." Always remember that your English Language Learners are:

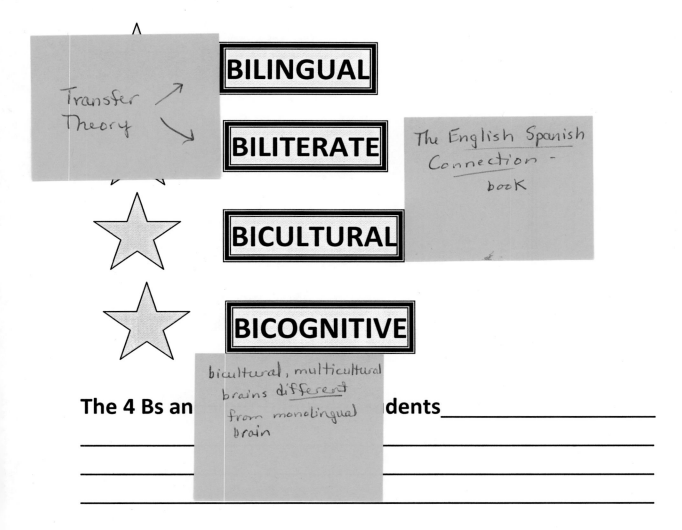

Transfer Theory

BILINGUAL

BILITERATE

The English Spanish Connection - book

BICULTURAL

BICOGNITIVE

bicultural, multicultural brains different from monolingual brain

The 4 Bs an_____dents_____

_____

_____

_____

3

Introduction

NO CHILD LEFT BEHIND NATIONAL READING PANEL'S RECOMMENDATIONS

The following mnemonic exercise will help you remember the National Reading Panel's 5 recommendations for improving reading in American schools.

1. Trace your hand below.

2. Write 1 recommendation in each finger. The 5 recommendations from the National Reading Panel are PHONICS, PHONEMIC AWARENESS, FLUENCY, VOCABULARY INSTRUCTION, AND READING COMPREHENSION.

WRITE YOUR DEFINITIONS

Reading Comprehension: My present definition_____

_____

_____

_____

My updated definition_____

_____

_____

_____

Vocabulary Development: My present definition_____

_____

_____

_____

My updated definition_____

_____

_____

_____

Fluency: My present definition_____

_____

_____

_____

My updated definition_____

_____

_____

_____

NO CHILD LEFT BEHIND
NATIONAL READING PANEL'S
RECOMMENDATIONS
PHONICS

"Phonics instruction is a way of teaching reading that stresses learning how letters correspond to sounds and how to use this knowledge in reading and spelling."

National Reading Panel

Phonics instruction and the bilingual student:_____

_____

_____

_____

_____

_____

_____

_____

_____

_____

_____

_____

PHONEMIC AWARENESS

Phonemes are the smallest units making up spoken language. English consists of about 41 phonemes. Phonemes combine to form syllables and words. Phonemic awareness refers to the ability to focus on and manipulate these phonemes in spoken words. Children develop phonemic awareness as they learn to segment, manipulate, and blend spoken language in these 5 ways:

1. **Blend** individual sounds to form a word.

2. **Isolate a** sound in a word.

3. **Match** sounds to words.

4. **Substitute** sounds in a word.

5. **Segment** a word into its constituent sounds.

Vocabulary refers to the words we must know to communicate effectively. In general, vocabulary can be described as oral vocabulary or reading vocabulary."

Researchers refer to 4 types of vocabulary

1. **Listening vocabulary**

2. **Speaking vocabulary**

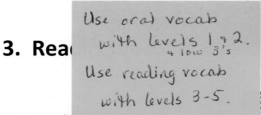

Use oral vocab with levels 1 & 2. & low 3's Use reading vocab with levels 3-5.

3. **Rea**

4. **Writ**

Vocabulary development and the bil

AEL - Academic English Language

Dolce - 220 high frequency words
Content area vocabulary

_____

_____

_____

_____

NO CHILD LEFT BEHIND
NATIONAL READING PANEL'S RECOMMENDATIONS
FLUENCY

Fluency is the ability to read effectively, and it involves 3 components:

1. Reading rate

2. Word recognition

3. Prosody (ability to read expressively, with appropriate phrasing and intonation)

(Rasinski, T., 2000; Richards, M. 2000)

Fluency and the bilingual student_____

_____

_____

_____

_____

NO CHILD LEFT BEHIND
NATIONAL READING PANEL'S
RECOMMENDATIONS
COMPREHENSION

"Comprehension is a creative multifaceted process in which students engage with the text."
Tierney, 1990

Three factors influence comprehension:

1. **The reader**

2. **The text**

3. **The purpose**

Comprehension and the bilingual student_____

_____

_____

_____

LANGUAGE PROFICIENCY AND PLACEMENT ASSESSMENTS ALWAYS LEAD THE PARADE!

Why do we give English language proficiency and placement assessments to our bilingual students?

I_____

I_____

I_____

What I learned _____

_____

_____

COMPREHENSIBLE INPUT

Dr. Stephen Krashen (1981) refers to "comprehensible input" as the understandable linguistic input required for successful second language acquisition. This theory refers to input that is just a level above the English Language Learner's second language acquisition level and therefore understood. The formula of "i+1 represents comprehensible input where the "i" stands for what the learner knows and the "+1" represents input one level above their current language acquisition level.

Input to be comprehensible must have the following characteristics:

1. Context clues such as experiences, situations, and concrete referents.

2. Paralinguistic clues such as gestures, facial expressions, and total use of body language.

3. Linguistic modifications such as intonation, repetition, paraphrasing, reduction in rate of speech, syntactic and vocabulary simplifications.

4. Structures and vocabulary already known to the students, together with some language not yet acquired is referred to as "input + 1." Dr. Krashen recommends that we take student's current level of language competence ("i") and increase the input by introducing language input which contains new language structures that are just beyond the student's current level of competence("+1").

5. Culturally relevant and meaningful content which is enough to connect to the English Language Learner's prior knowledge.

THE LANGUAGE ACQUISITION AND LITERACY CONNECTION

"Dr. Jim Cummin's distinction between two types of language: basic interpersonal communications skills (BICS) and cognitive academic language proficiency (CALP) has directly influenced classroom instruction. Research has shown that the average student can develop conversational fluency within 2-5 years, but that developing fluency in more technical, academic language can take from 4-7 years depending on many variables such as language proficiency level, age and time of arrival at school, level of academic proficiency in the native language, and the degree of support for achieving academic proficiency (Cummins, 1981, 1996; Hakuta, Butler, & Witt, 2000; Thomas & Collier, 1997)."

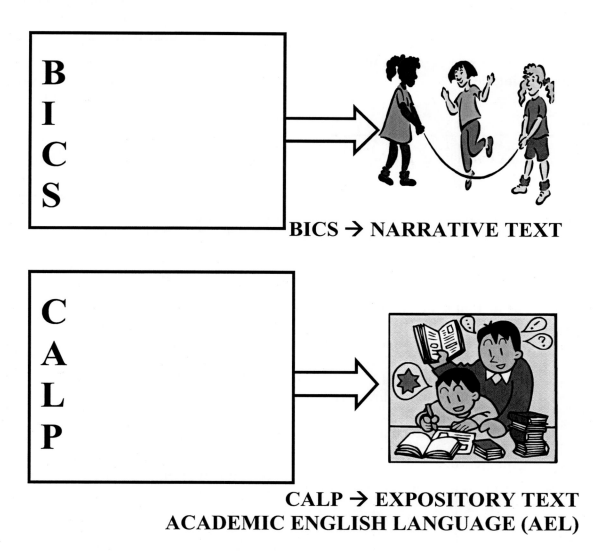

B I C S

BICS → NARRATIVE TEXT

C A L P

CALP → EXPOSITORY TEXT
ACADEMIC ENGLISH LANGUAGE (AEL)

NARRATIVE AND EXPOSITORY TEXTS
A COMPARISON OF TEXT FEATURES

NARRATIVE TEXT	EXPOSITORY TEXT
Fiction in which values are used to describe and/or explain human behavior. A text that tells a story. An account of events.	Non-fiction written by authors to inform, explain, describe, present information or to persuade. Information can be verified as true.
Theme-based text which may be directly stated or implied.	Fact and information-based text using clear and precise dialogue. Various text patterns are signaled by different headings, subheadings, and signal words.
Emotional Connection: Intends to entertain.	Emotional Connection: Intends to inform.

Narrative text characteristics:
1. Well-developed characters who may use dialogue
2. Carefully fashioned plot with a problem and resolution.
3. Theme that explains the meaning of the story.
4. Setting describes where or when the story takes place.
5. Involves a setting and a character(s) who are involved in one or more conflicts (e.g., interpersonal, internal, with society).
6. Includes events, actions, behaviors.
7. May be written in first, second, or third person.
	Expository Text Characteristics:
	1. Heller (1995) identifies 7 basic expository text structures:
	    1. definition
	    2. description
	    3. process
	    4. classification
	    5. comparison
	    6. analysis
	    7. persuasion
	
	2. To inform, explain, describe, enumerate, discuss, compare/contrast, and problem-solve.
	
	3. Subject oriented focused on a specific topic.

Narrative Text Structure: **Beginning: Contains setting, characters, problem(s), initiating events.** **Middle:** Turning points, crisis, rising action, climax, subplot. **End:** Resolution, falling action, ending.	**Expository Text Structure:** The structure or organization is dependent upon the form or genre i.e. brochure, editorial, letter, map, brochure. Structures may include definition, description, process (scientific process, collection, time order, or listing) classification, cause/effect, compare/contrast, problem/solution, sequence, analysis, and persuasion.
Narrative Text Types: Biographies, drama, diaries, excerpts from novels, fables, fantasies, folk tales, historical fiction, legends, mysteries, myths, novels, personal narratives, plays, poetry, mysteries, science fiction, short stories, sitcoms, tall tales, etc.	**Expository Text Types:** Content area textbooks, autobiographies, biographies, book reports, cartoons, catalogs, charts, definitions, essays, forms, graphs, government documents, essays, interviews, invitations, journals, lists, newspaper and magazine articles, maps and directions, recounts of an event, research papers, speeches, tables, worksheets, etc.
Uses illustrations to extend text meaning.	**Uses illustrations to clarify or explain.**
Concrete concepts related to experiences.	**Abstract content area/topic related concepts.**

AFFECTIVE FILTER

Dr. Stephen Krashen's Affective Filter hypotheses suggests that an individual's emotions can directly interfere or assist in the learning of a new language.

According to Krashen, "learning a new language is different from learning other subjects because it requires public practice. Speaking out in a new language can result in anxiety, embarrassment, and anger. These negative emotions can create a kind of filter that blocks the learner's ability to process new or difficult words. Classrooms that are fully engaging, non-threatening, and affirming of a child's native language and cultural heritage can have a direct effect on the student's ability to learn by increasing motivation and encouraging risk taking."

Source: Reed, Bracken, and Railsback, Jennifer. Strategies and Resources for Mainstream Teachers of English Language Learners, Bracken Reed. Portland, OR: Northwest Regional Educational Laboratory, 2003.

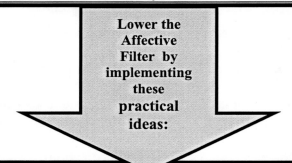

Lower the Affective Filter by implementing these practical ideas:

1. Create a productive and inclusive learning environment by creating a safe environment in which the student's primary language and culture are genuinely valued, respected, and used as a foundation for all curriculum and instruction .

2. Help your English Language Learners and their families feel welcome by creating a "Cheers School" environment. Do you remember the TV show Cheers theme song - "Where everybody knows your name and everybody's glad your came." This is the message all ELL and their families should feel when they come to our schools and classrooms. Implement Jo's *Welcome To Our School Video/DVD* idea to achieve this feeling the moment these families register their children at your school.

3. Integrate Jo Gusman's *Language Buddy Club* idea to help you properly prepare your English speaking students to assist you, and provide additional support to your English Language Learners.

4. Make your input comprehensible at all times.

5. Implement "teach me how to learn" and cooperative learning structures in your daily instruction. This will empower the ELL with the structures, patterns, and processes needed to succeed in all formal and informal school activities.

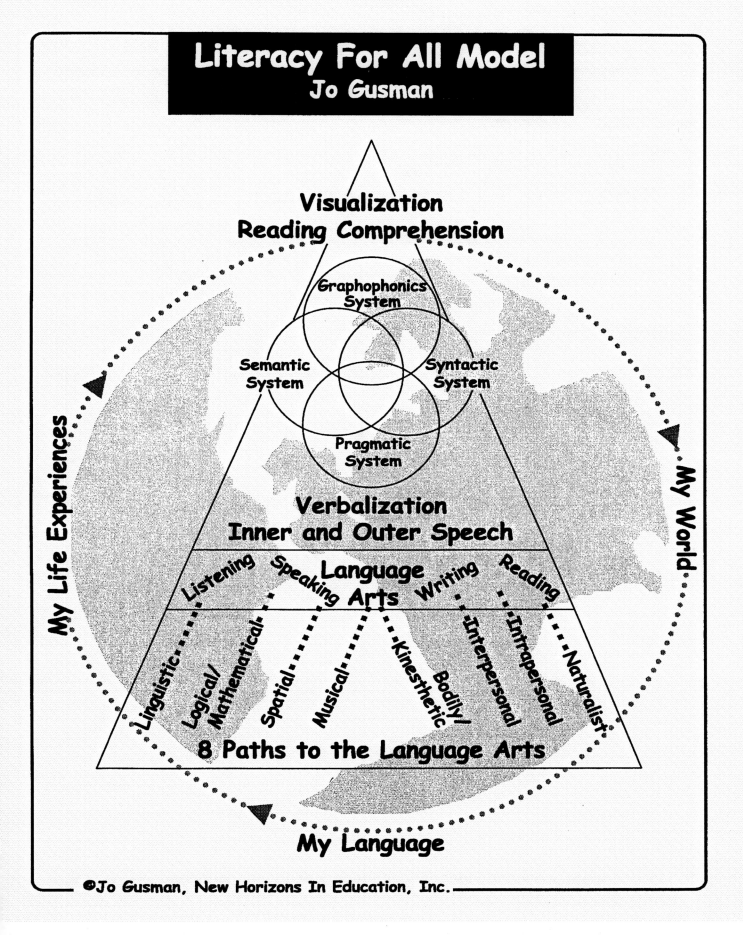

Literacy For All Model
Jo Gusman

Visualization
Reading Comprehension

Graphophonics System

Semantic System

Syntactic System

Pragmatic System

Verbalization
Inner and Outer Speech

My Life Experiences

My World

Listening   Speaking   Language   Writing   Reading
Arts

Linguistic   Logical/Mathematical   Spatial   Musical   Kinesthetic   Bodily!   Interpersonal   Intrapersonal   Naturalist

8 Paths to the Language Arts

My Language

©Jo Gusman, New Horizons In Education, Inc.

THE FOUR CUEING SYSTEMS

"Language is a complex system for creating meaning through socially shared conventions (Halliday, 1978). English like other languages, involves four cueing systems."

PHONOLOGICAL/ GRAPHOPHONIC-→SOUND SYSTEM	SYNTACTIC →STRUCTURAL SYSTEM
SEMANTIC →MEANING SYSTEM	**PRAGMATIC →SOCIAL AND CULTURAL USE SYSTEM**

BRAIN-BASED INTEGRATED ELA/ELD CONTENT AREA LESSON

STEP 1: Mindfully Explore the Reading Material Before You Write Your Lesson Plan

Content Area: _____

Topic: _____ **Standard:**_____

VOCABULARY DEVELOPMENT USING THE BRAIN'S 6 PATTERNS	"BEING THERE" EXPERIENCES THAT LEAD TO COMPREHENSION	CONCEPT DEVELOPMENT OPPORTUNITIES	SKILL DEVELOPMENT OPPORTUNITIES
OBJECTS:			
ACTIONS:			
PROCEDURES:			
SYSTEMS:			
RELATIONSHIPS:			
SITUATIONS:			

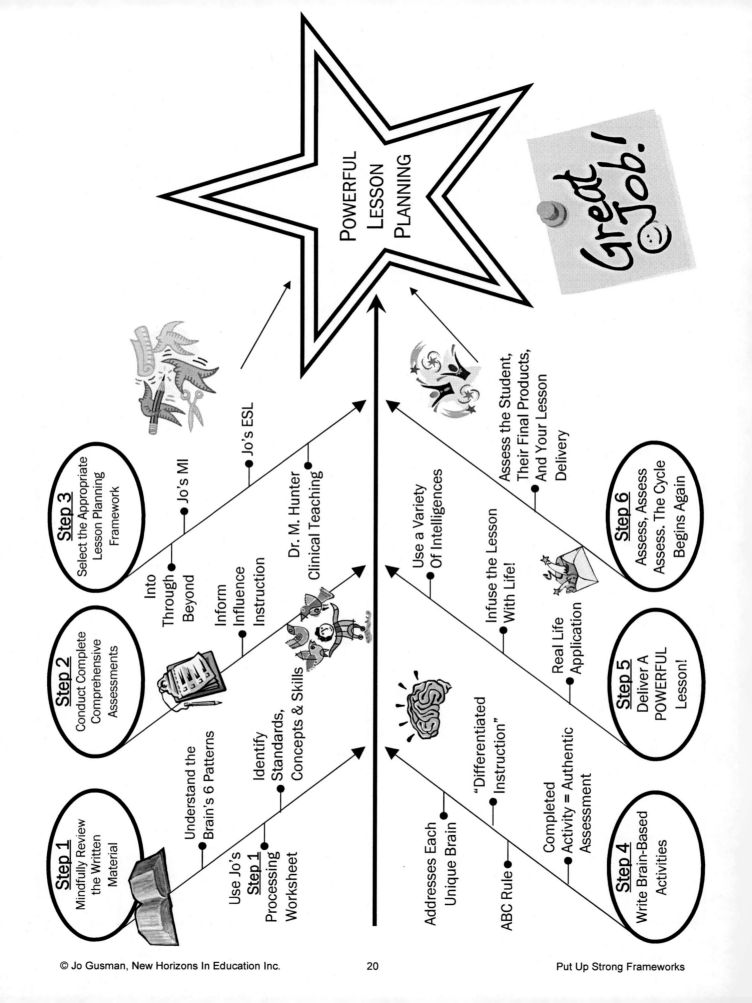

POWERFUL LESSON PLANNING

Great Job!

Step 1
Mindfully Review the Written Material

Understand the Brain's 6 Patterns

Use Jo's **Step 1** Processing Worksheet

Identify Standards, Concepts & Skills

Step 2
Conduct Complete Comprehensive Assessments

Step 3
Select the Appropriate Lesson Planning Framework

Into
Through
Beyond

Jo's MI

Jo's ESL

Inform
Influence
Instruction

Dr. M. Hunter
Clinical Teaching

Use a Variety Of Intelligences

Assess the Student, Their Final Products, And Your Lesson Delivery

Infuse the Lesson With Life!

Real Life Application

Addresses Each Unique Brain

"Differentiated Instruction"

Completed Activity = Authentic Assessment

ABC Rule

Step 4
Write Brain-Based Activities

Step 5
Deliver A POWERFUL Lesson!

Step 6
Assess, Assess, Assess. The Cycle Begins Again

Put Up Strong Frameworks

Multiple Paths to Success

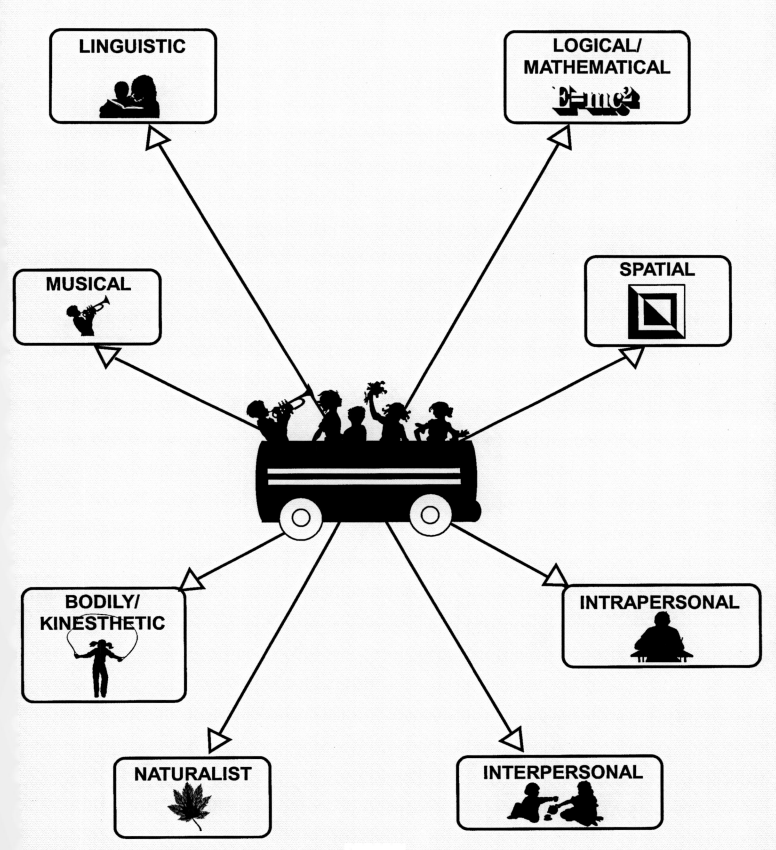

Jo Gusman, New Horizons in Education

8success.pm6

Las Inteligencias Múltiples

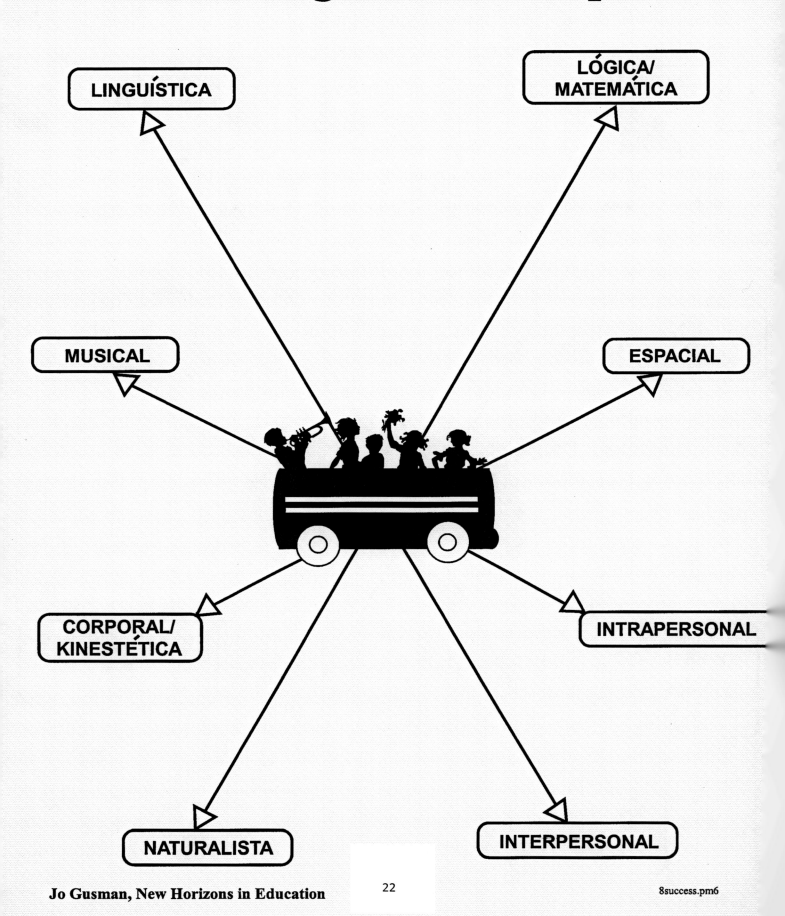

LINGUÍSTICA

LÓGICA/
MATEMÁTICA

MUSICAL

ESPACIAL

CORPORAL/
KINESTÉTICA

INTRAPERSONAL

NATURALISTA

INTERPERSONAL

HAVE A GREAT TIME!

"MULTIPLE PATHS TO SUCCESS" LESSON PLAN

THEME: _____

BOOK TITLE: _____

STANDARD/CONCEPTUAL FOCUS: _____

SKILL DEVELOPMENT OPPORTUNITY:_____

MULTIPLE INTELLIGENCES OPPORTUNITIES

INTELLIGENCES	ACTIVITIES
LINGUISTIC	
LOGICAL /MATHEMATICAL	
SPATIAL	
MUSICAL	
BODILY/KINESTHETIC	
INTERPERSONAL	
INTRAPERSONAL	
NATURALIST	

Multiple Intelligences  Book of Activities

Created by Jo Gusman

A
- ★ABC Big Book
- ★Jo's ABC's Of It All Game
- ★Ads
- ★Advertisements
- ★Advertising Folders
- ★Advice Columns
- ★Allegory
- ★Album
- ★Art Gallery Display
- ★Anagram
- ★Anecdotes
- ★Anthems
- ★Apology Letter
- ★Appeal
- ★Appendices
- ★Application Form
- ★Articles
- ★Autobiography
- ★Awards
- ★Award Ceremony

B
- ★Ballad
- ★Banner
- ★Batik
- ★Beauty Tip Article
- ★Bed Time Story
- ★Big Book
- ★Billboard
- ★Biography
- ★Birth Certificate
- ★Blueprint
- ★Blurbs
- ★Book Jackets
- ★Book Review
- ★Book
- ★Brochure
- ★Bulletin
- ★Bulletin Board
- ★Bumper Sticker
- ★Business Card

C
- ★Calendar
- ★Captions
- ★Card Game
- ★Cartoon
- ★Catalog Description
- ★Ceramic
- ★Cereal Boxes
- ★Certificates
- ★Chants
- ★Character Sketches
- ★Cinquain
- ★Collection
- ★Comic Books
- ★Comic Strip
- ★Commercial Product
- ★Comparison Chart
- ★Cookbook
- ★Complaint Form
- ★Computer Program
- ★Constitution
- ★Consumer Guide
- ★Contract
- ★Costume
- ★Couplet
- ★Court Case
- ★Coupon
- ★Critic
- ★Critique
- ★Crossword Puzzle
- ★Cumulative Story

D
- ★Dance
- ★Debate
- ★Definitions
- ★Descriptions
- ★Description of scenes
- ★Detective Work
- ★Diagram
- ★Dialogues
- ★Diary
- ★Diorama
- ★Dictionary
- ★Diet Plan
- ★Digest
- ★Directions
- ★Directory
- ★Display
- ★Documents
- ★ "Doodles From the Desk of _____ "
- ★Drama
- ★Dramatic Monolog
- ★Dream Analysis
- ★Dream Journal

E

- ★Ecology Article
- ★Ecology Bumper Sticker
- ★Ecology Poster
- ★Editorial
- ★Elegy
- ★E-Mail
- ★Encyclopedia Entry
- ★Ending to Story
- ★Environmental Handbook
- ★Epilogue
- ★Epitaph
- ★Essay
- ★Etching
- ★Evaluations
- ★Experiment Record

F

- ★Fashion Show
- ★Film Strip
- ★First Aid Kit
- ★First Aid Procedure
- ★Flag
- ★Floral Arrangement
- ★Folktale
- ★Fortune Cookie Fortunes

G

- ★Game
- ★Game Show
- ★Game Show Rules
- ★Garden
- ★Glossary
- ★Good News/Bad News Story
- ★Gossip Column
- ★Graph
- ★Graphic Design
- ★Graphic Organizer
- ★Greeting Card
- ★Grocery List
- ★Guest Book
- ★Guest Lists
- ★Guest Speaker

H

- ★Haiku
- ★Handbill
- ★Headline
- ★Honor Ceremony
- ★Horoscope
- ★Hospital Brochure
- ★Hot Seat
- ★House Plans
- ★House Plant Guide
- ★"How to" Pamphlet

I

- ★Idea Map
- ★Illustration
- ★Illustrated Story
- ★Impressionistic Art
- ★Impromptu Speech
- ★Improvisation
- ★Index
- ★Inquiry Activity
- ★Inspirational Speech
- ★Instructional Handbook
- ★Interview
- ★Introductory Letter
- ★Introductory Offer
- ★Invitation

J

- ★Jingle
- ★Job Application
- ★Joke
- ★Jump Rope Chant
- ★Junk Mail
- ★Journal

K

- ★Kabuki Drama
- ★Kaleidoscope
- ★Keepsake
- ★Keystone Cop Comedy
- ★Kite Making
- ★Knighthood Ceremony
- ★Knit
- ★Knot Making Contest
- ★Kudos

L
- ★ Label
- ★ Legend
- ★ Lesson
- ★ Letter to the Editor
- ★ Letters (Calligraphy)
- ★ License Plate
- ★ Life Map
- ★ Limerick
- ★ List
- ★ Logo
- ★ Love Letter
- ★ Love Note
- ★ Lullaby
- ★ Lyric

M
- ★ Magazine Article
- ★ Magazine Ad
- ★ Magazine
- ★ Map
- ★ Map Legend
- ★ Marquee
- ★ Matchbook
- ★ Memory Book
- ★ Menu
- ★ Metaphor
- ★ Mission Statement
- ★ Mobile
- ★ Model
- ★ Money
- ★ Monograph
- ★ Monologue
- ★ Monster Tale
- ★ Montage
- ★ Movie Review
- ★ Movie Script
- ★ Movie Title
- ★ Mural
- ★ Museum Exhibit
- ★ Mystery

N
- ★ Name
- ★ News Analysis
- ★ Newscast
- ★ Newsletter
- ★ Newspaper Advertisement
- ★ Newspaper Article
- ★ Newspaper Feature
- ★ Newspaper Headline
- ★ Newspaper
- ★ Nonsense Words
- ★ Notes
- ★ Number Booklet
- ★ Nursery Rhyme

O
- ★ Obituary
- ★ Observation Log
- ★ Odes
- ★ Oil Painting
- ★ Opinion
- ★ Oral Report
- ★ Outdoor Games
- ★ Outline

P
- ★ Package
- ★ Package for a Specific Product
- ★ Palindrome
- ★ Pamphlet
- ★ Pantomime
- ★ Paper Weight
- ★ Paragraph
- ★ Parable
- ★ Parodies
- ★ Party Tips
- ★ Pastel Drawings
- ★ Patterns
- ★ Patterns Books
- ★ Peace Treaty
- ★ Perfect Party Location Catalog
- ★ Personal Ad
- ★ Persuasion
- ★ Persuasive Letter
- ★ Photo Album
- ★ Photo Essay
- ★ Photograph
- ★ Photo Exhibit
- ★ Pictorial Letter
- ★ Picture Book/Dictionary
- ★ Picturesque Phrases
- ★ Play
- ★ Pledge
- ★ Poem
- ★ Portrait
- ★ Postcard
- ★ Poster
- ★ Pottery
- ★ Problem Solving
- ★ Product Descriptions
- ★ Profound Sayings
- ★ Prologue
- ★ Propaganda
- ★ Proposal
- ★ Protection Handbook

P
- ★ Protest Letter
- ★ Protest Signs
- ★ Proverb
- ★ Puns
- ★ Puppet Show
- ★ Puzzles

Q
- ★ Qualification Letter
- ★ Questions
- ★ Questionnaires
- ★ Quips
- ★ Quiz
- ★ Quiz Show
- ★ Quotes

R
- ★ Radio Show
- ★ Ransom Note
- ★ Reaction Papers
- ★ Reader's Theater
- ★ Real Estate Notice
- ★ Rebuttal
- ★ Recipe Book
- ★ Recipe Card
- ★ Record Cover
- ★ Reference File
- ★ Relief Map
- ★ Remedies
- ★ Reports
- ★ Requests
- ★ Requiems
- ★ Requisition
- ★ Resume
- ★ Reviews
- ★ Revisions
- ★ Riddle
- ★ Rock and Roll Song
- ★ Role Playing
- ★ Roller Skating
- ★ Round Robin Reading
- ★ Rubber Stamping
- ★ Rubbing
- ★ Rubric

S
- ★ Sand Casting
- ★ Sales Notices
- ★ Sales Pitches
- ★ Satire
- ★ Schedules
- ★ Science Calendars
- ★ Science Fiction
- ★ Scrapbooks
- ★ Scripts
- ★ Scrolls
- ★ Sculpture
- ★ Secret Garden
- ★ Self Description
- ★ Sentence Fragment
- ★ Sentences
- ★ Sequel
- ★ Serial
- ★ Sermon
- ★ Short Stories
- ★ Signs
- ★ Silk Screening
- ★ Silly Sayings
- ★ Skits
- ★ Slide Show
- ★ Slogan
- ★ Small Scale Drawing
- ★ Soap Operas
- ★ Society Pages
- ★ Song Lyrics
- ★ Song Collection Index
- ★ Sonnet
- ★ Space Story
- ★ Speeches
- ★ Spoofs
- ★ Spooky Tales
- ★ Sportscast
- ★ Sports Page
- ★ Statement
- ★ Stencil
- ★ Stitchery
- ★ Story Beginning
- ★ Summary
- ★ Superstition
- ★ Survey

WANTED!

Multiple Intelligences A B C Book of Activities

Created by Jo Gusman

T

★Taped Message
★Table of Contents
★Tall Tale
★Telegram
★Telephone Book Ads

★Terrarium
★Textbook
★Thank You Card
★Theater Program
★Timeline

★Title
★Tongue Twister
★Traffic Regulations
★Traffic Sign
★Transparency for Overhead

★Travel Brochure
★Travel Folder
★Travelogue
★Travel Posters
★Travel Tour Package

★Tribute
★Trivia
★T-Shirts
★TV Documentary
★TV Commercial

★TV Infomercial
★TV Guide
★TV Newscast
★TV Program/Sitcom

U

★Ultimatum
★UNICEF Donation
★UNICEF Participation
★Underline Main Ideas
★Uniform
★Union Catalog
★Union Guidelines

★Union Label
★Unite Diverse Groups
★United Nations Study
★University Tour
★Unpack
★Unscramble Code
★Unscramble Word

★Upholstery
★Upside-down Cake
★Used Car Ads
★Usher
★Urban Study

V

★Venn Diagram
★Video
★Video Game

★Value Statement
★Vocabulary List
★Vignettes

★Vita

W

★Walking Tour
★Want Ads
★Wanted Poster
★Warning Signs
★Watercolor Painting

★Weather Report
★Web Site
★Wills
★Wise Sayings
★Wish List

★Word Problems
★Word Portraits
★Written Reports

X

★Xerography
★X-Ray
★Xylograph

★Xylophone

Put Up Strong Lesson Planning Frameworks

Y	★Yacht Race	★Yardstick	★Yearbook
	★Yacht Club Rules	★Yarn Craft	★Yellow Pages
	★Yard Sale	★"Yarn Spin"	★Yogurt
	★Yard Sale	★Year Calendar	★Yoga
Z	★Zagat Restaurant Guide	★Zoological Study	
	★Zone Study	★Zoometry	

CREATING MI STUDENT PORTFOLIOS

Use the Multiple Intelligences theory to organize a student's portfolio. This will allow the student to express their knowledge in various ways.

☐ **LINGUISTIC**
WRITTEN DESCRIPTION OF INVESTIGATIONS
JOURNAL ENTRIES
AUDIO CASSETTE RECORDING IN L1 & L2
LETTERS
ESSAYS
REPORTS
READING LOGS
WRITING SAMPLES USING VARIOUS WRITING DOMAINS
LISTS OF THEIR FAVORITE BOOKS
"WHAT I HAVE LEARNED THIS MONTH" TABLE OF CONTENTS
ANECDOTAL RECORDS
EVALUATION OF AN ORAL LANGUAGE PRESENTATION
STUDENT PROFILE
BRAINSTORM LIST OF IDEAS

☐ **LOGICAL-MATHEMATICAL**
GRAPHIC REPRESENTATIONS
DIAGRAMS OF PROBLEM SOLVING PROCESSES
CHECKLISTS
TRADITIONAL TESTS - VARIOUS TEST FORMATS
WORKSHEETS
CHARTS
SKILL CHECKLISTS
PROBLEM-SOLVING PROCESSING SHEETS

☐ **SPATIAL**
GRAPHIC ORGANIZERS   "LEARNING QUILT"
PUZZLES   VISUALIZATION DRAWING
PICTURE CARDS   VIDEOS/SLIDE SHOW
PHOTOS   DRAWINGS
ANY AND ALL ARTISTIC REPRESENTATIONS

☐ <u>MUSICAL</u>

SONGS, RAPS, JINGLES, CHANTS THE STUDENT HAS WRITTEN
   AND PERFORMED
POEMS, LIMMERICKS, RIDDLES

☐ <u>BODILY/KINESTHETIC</u>

VIDEO OF PLAYS, READERS THEATER, ROLE-PLAYING
GAMES DESIGNED BY THE STUDENT
ALL WHOLE-BODY ACTIVITIES

☐ <u>INTERPERSONAL</u>

PHOTOS OR VIDEOS OF STUDENT WORKING IN COOPERATIVE
   LEARNING GROUPS
RECORDINGS OF GROUP DISCUSSIONS
PROJECTS THAT SHOW STUDENT'S "GROUP SMART"
GROUP REPORTS

☐ <u>INTRAPERSONAL</u>

EVIDENCE OF SELF REFLECTION AND SELF-KNOWLEDGE
JOURNAL ENTRIES
IMAGERY DRAWINGS
QUESTIONNAIRES ON ATTITUDES TOWARD A PARTICULAR
   ASSIGNMENT OR CONTENT AREA

☐ <u>NATURALIST</u>

OBSERVATION JOURNALS
COLLECTIONS
CLASSIFICATION SYSTEM
SCRAPBOOK
ALL ASSIGNMENTS WHICH CONNECT THE
      CONCEPT/SKILL TO BE LEARNED TO NATURE,
         THE REAL WORLD, AND THEIR CULTURAL CONTEXT

MULTIPLE INTELLIGENCES THEORY RESOURCES

BOOK

Armstrong, T. *Multiple Intelligences in the Classroom*. Alexandria, VA: ASCD, 1994. (In Spanish and English)

Campbell, B. *The Multiple Intelligences Handbook. Lesson Plans and More*. Stanwood, WA: Campbell & Associates, Inc. 1994.

Chapman, C. & Freeman, L. *Multiple Intelligences Centers and Projects*. Arlington Heights, IL: IRI/Skylight Training and Publishing, Inc., 1996.

Gardner, Howard. *Frames of Mind. The Theory of Multiple Intelligences*. New York, NY: Basic Books, 1983.

Gardner, Howard. *Multiple Intelligences. The Theory in Practice*. New York, NY: Basic Books, 1993.

Gusman, Jo. *Multiple Intelligences and the English Language Learner. A Resource Handbook*. Sacramento, CA: New Horizons in Education, Inc., 2002.

Kagan, S. & Kagan, M. *Multiple Intelligences: The Complete MI Book*. San Clemente, CA: Kagan Cooperative Learning, 1998.

Teele, S. *The Multiple Intelligences School: A Place for All Students To Succeed*. Redlands, CA: Sue Teele and Associates, 1997.

Teele, S. *Rainbows of Intelligence*. Redlands, CA: Sue Teele and Associates, 1997.

ASSESSMENT TOOLS

Bellanca, J., Chapman, C. & Swartz, E. Multiple Assessments for Multiple Intelligences. Arlington Heights, Il: IRI/Skylight Training and Publishing, Inc., 1994.

Lazear, D. Multiple Intelligences Approaches to Assessment. Solving the Assessment Conundrum. Tucson, AZ: Zephyr, 1994.

Teele, S. The Teele Inventory of Multiple Intelligences. Redlands, CA: Sue Teele and Associates.

VIDEOS

Armstrong,T., Gusman, J., Teele, S.   Multiple Intelligences: Discovering the Giftedness in ALL. Port Chester, NY: National Professional Resources, Inc., 1997.
*Includes interviews with Dr. Sue Teele, Jo Gusman, and several teachers, administrators and authors who share their views and experiences with the Multiple Intelligences theory.)
(Spanish and English version available through New Horizons In Education, Inc., (916) 482-4405)

Gardner, Howard. Optimizing Intelligences: Thinking, Emotion and Creativity. Port Chester, NY: National Professional Resources, Inc., 1998. *Includes interviews with Mihaly Csikszentmihalyi, Daniel Goleman, Peter Salovey, Renilde Montessori, Maurice Elias, Jo Gusman.
(Spanish and English version available through New Horizons In Education, Inc., (916) 482-4405)

Gardner, H.   How Are Kids Smart? Multiple Intelligences in the Classroom. Gloucester, MA: National Professional Resources, Inc., 1995.) (Spanish and English version available through New Horizons In Education Inc., (916) 482-4405)

Gusman, Jo. Multiple Intelligences and the Second Language Learner. Port Chester, NY: National Professional Resources, Inc., 1998.)
(Spanish and English version available through New Horizons In Education, Inc., (916) 482-4405)

Gusman, Jo. Differentiated Instruction and The English Language Learner. Port Chester, NY: National Professional Resources, Inc., 2004.) (Available through New Horizons In Education, Inc., (916) 482-4405)

Kagan, S. and Kagan, L. Cooperative Learning and Multiple Intelligences, Elementary, Middle School and High School. Sandy, UT: The LPD Video Journal of Education, 1998. (3 different grade level specific videos)

Lazear, D. MI in Action: Your School and the Multiple Intelligences.
5 Video Set. Tucson, AZ: Zephyr Press, 1995.

Teele, Sue. Rainbows of Intelligence: Raising Student Performance Through Multiple Intelligences. Port Chester, NY: National Professional Resources, Inc., 2000. (Spanish and English version available through New Horizons In Education, Inc., (916) 482-4405.

WEB SITES

Dr. Sue Teele and Associates   www.sueteele.com

Educational Leadership: Teaching For Multiple Intelligences
        http://www.ascd.org/publications/ed_lead/199709/toc.html

Ed Web   http://www.edwebproject.org/
        www.edwebproject.org/edref.mi.intro.html

Multiple Intelligences for Adult Literacy and Adult Education
        http://literacyworks.org/mi/home.html

Multiple Intelligences Developmental Assessment Scale
        http://www.miresearch.org

Multiple Intelligences and Learning Styles
        www.casacanada.com/mulin.html

Multiple Intelligences: A Theory for Everyone
        www.education-world.com/a_curr/curr054.shtml

Multiple Intelligences: It's Not How Smart You Are. It's How You're Smart
        www.education-world.com/a_curr/curr207.shtm

Project Zero, at the Harvard Graduate School of Education
http://www.pz.harvard.edu/index.cfm

Tapping Into Multiple Intelligences
http://www.thirteen.org/edonline/concept2class/

Technology and Multiple Intelligences   www.eduscapes.com/tap/topic68.htm

The Gardner School   www.gardnerschool.org

The Tool Room: About Howard Gardner – Theory of Multiple Intelligences
http://www.newhorizons.org/future/Creating_the_Future/crfut_gardner.html

Thomas Armstrong   www.thomasarmstrong.com/multiple_intelligences.htm

PLANNING AN ESL/ELD LESSON: SOME RECOMMENDED STEPS

☑	
	LESSON TITLE:
	CONCEPT/SKILL-"TRANSFER BRIDGE CONNECTION": (What concept do you want to teach in this lesson? How will you connect this skill or concept to the role students have in their family, their prior knowledge, and real world application?)
	STANDARDS/OBJECTIVES/GOALS: (What will the students be able to do at the end of this lesson?) Select these goals and objectives from your district and state guidelines. 1. 2. 3.
	VOCABULARY (What vocabulary must the students understand? How will you teach the vocabulary words so that all ESL students understand?)

☑	**"BEING THERE" EXPERIENCES:** (Where can you take the students so they have a meaningful context for this lesson?) 1. 2.
	SETTING THE STAGE: (How will you arrange the room? What do you need to create a context-filled environment?)
	MULTI-SENSORY PROPS: (What instructional materials will you need to stimulate all of the senses?)
	PEOPLE RESOURCES: (Who can you bring in to assist, support or teach this lesson?)

☑	LESSON DELIVERY
	"ANTICIPATORY SET": (Hook them into your lesson! Act it out, sing it, bring in a surprise guest - be creative!)
	OBJECTIVES/PURPOSE: (Why do they need to learn this? What does this have to do with <u>their</u> lives?)
	DIRECTED INSTRUCTION : (Bring your lesson to life by using the multiple intelligences throughout your directed instruction.)
	"PROCESS THE EXPERIENCE" TIME (Teacher directed processing time: checking for understanding, reflection, pair-share, journal time, clarification requests, confirmation checks, group-share, Language Buddies.)

☑	
	TEACHER DEMONSTRATION/MODELING (Teacher models any activity students will be doing. Teacher demonstrates task analysis of activity to be completed by students.)
	CHECKING FOR UNDERSTANDING: (Do the students understand how to do the activity? How will they tell you they understand if they can not speak English? How could they show you they understand?)
	GUIDED PRACTICE: (What cooperative learning structures might you use? Which intelligences are the students using?) (Teacher serves as guide/facilitator) (*DECISION POINT! DO YOU NEED TO RETEACH? GIVE INDIVIDUALIZED HELP?)
	INDEPENDENT PRACTICE: (What activities will you assign to insure understanding? Which intelligences are the students using? Can the students choose from a variety of activities? Can you send home a cassette of your directed instruction? Can you send home bilingual support materials?)

ASSESSMENT: (How will the students <u>show</u> you they understand the concept you taught? What would be the most <u>authentic</u> way to assess your students?)

LEARNING CELEBRATION: (How will you show the students that you have come full circle in the lesson? How will the teacher and the students celebrate their successes? How will you process the complete lesson?)

INTO→THROUGH→BEYOND READING PROCESS AND LESSON PLANNING FRAMEWORK

INTO

Introduce activities that help the students draw upon their prior knowledge, thus creating a readiness for the reading selection. Give students time to reflect and to bring their experiences and questions the text. These activities are intended to motivate, excite, and empower the students to be successful meaning makers and readers.

SET THE PURPOSE FOR READING

EXPLICITLY EXPLAIN FORMAT, PATTERNS, IN THE TEXTBOOK CHAPTER.

EXPLICITLY MODEL TEXTBOOK LITERACY PROCESSES, STRATEGIES, AND SKILLS

PREDICTION ACTIVITIES

DISCUSSION

QUICKWRITE

ROLE-PLAYING

VISUALS (PICTURES, VIDEOS ETC.)

POETRY, SONGS

RELATED BOOKS/STORIES

* Language Experience Approach

THROUGH

During this stage, select activities that focus on skill development opportunities. By setting the stage with INTO activities, students now have a context for the skills they will interact with, explore, and learn.

TELL BACKS

PARTNER READING

QUAKER READING

HOT SEAT

DOUBLE ENTRY JOURNAL

CHORAL READING

GRAPHIC ORGANIZERS

READER'S THEATER

WRITING

EXPLICITLY MODEL HOW TO USE SKILL DEVELOPMENT WORKSHEETS

BEYOND

It's time to integrate the curriculum! These activities focus on the application of content and concepts learned through INTO AND THROUGH experiences. Students now experience the selection in a wide variety of disciplines.

THEMATIC UNITS

TABLEAU

WRITING→PUBLISHING

EXTENDED READING AND RESEARCH

CONTENT AREA INTEGRATION

SCRAPBOOKS

PHASE ONE - "INTO"
LEADING STUDENTS INTO THE TEXT

INTO activities should motivate, excite and empower students to be successful "meaning makers" and readers.

Introduce activities which help students draw upon <u>their</u> prior knowledge.

Give students time to reflect and to bring their understanding to the selection.

INTO ACTIVITIES

LISTENING/SPEAKING FOCUS
PREDICTION
DISCUSSIONS
BRAINSTORMING/CLUSTERING
SPATIAL- FILMS, PICTURES, ART
SONGS
ROLE PLAY
DIRECTED PICTURE THINKING
INTRAPERSONAL REFLECTION TIME
QUICKWRITE

THROUGH ACTIVITIES

CHORAL READING
GRAPHIC ORGANIZERS
COOPERATIVE LEARNING JIGSAWS
VOCABULARY COLLECTING
VOCABULARY BUILDING
IDENTIFYING SOURCES
ILLUSTRATING QUOTATIONS,
CONCEPTS, AND SKILLS
PARAPHRASING
SENTENCE STRIP STORY EXPLORATION
"TELL BACKS"
"HOT SEAT"
WRITING PROCESS ACTIVITIES

PHASE TWO - "THROUGH"
ASSISTING STUDENTS THROUGH THE TEXT

THROUGH activities should help students unlock the author's meaning and message.

Help students make abstract ideas visual and concrete.

Having set the stage with INTO activities, students now have a context for the skills they will interact with, explore, and learn.

PHASE THREE- "BEYOND"
LEADING STUDENTS BEYOND THE TEXT

BEYOND activities help the students experience the story across the curriculum.

Select comprehension development activities that will help students apply what they have learned, in a "real world" context.

Explore content area concepts across the curriculum.

BEYOND ACTIVITIES

WRITING ACTIVITIES

EXTENDED READING

RESEARCH

ACROSS THE CURRICULUM
"REAL WORLD" APPLICATION
ACTIVITIES

"TABLEAU"

Reading is a multifaceted developmental process where the student learns to make connections between language, print, and thought. Thought includes the student's conceptual framework which has been shaped by his/her prior experiences, culture, and education. For a student to understand messages encoded in English print, they must bring to the text their primary language, decoding skills, language facility, conceptual frameworks, and thinking abilities, in order to understand the author's message. Thus, the effective teacher addresses all **four** areas important to reading comprehension:

1. **Decoding Skills/Word Recognition**
2. **Language Development/Competence**
3. **Concept/Context Building**
4. **Critical Thinking Skills and Strategies**
   (Sutton, 1989)

The English Language Student and Decoding Skills/Word Recognition Strategies

1. **Let's Talk About Phonics in Isolation!**
   English is not a phonetically consistent language. Teaching phonics in isolation, in English, to non-native English speakers can be quite confusing and frustrating. It also may be difficult for English Language Learners to differentiate sound variations in the English language especially if those sounds do not exist in their own language.

2. **Focus on Contextualized Language**
   Students at the early stages of second language acquisition may not be able to read aloud from an English reader, but they <u>CAN</u> understand words and symbols that are contextualized. Ask your students to bring you packaged grocery and household items from their home environment. Use these product labels to assess the decoding and word recognition skills and strategies your students already know and apply. These are the same strategies you can mindfully show them to use when they are decoding English text.

3. **Teach Me How To Read Using the "Patterns and Programs" My Brain Has Already Developed**
   Assess your students' literacy skills in their <u>primary</u> language, remembering that language is made up of 4 processes - listening, speaking, writing, and reading. Knowledge about their primary language and literacy development is your best friend when it comes to teaching them how to read in English.

HELPING ENGLISH LANGUAGE LEARNERS BECOME PROFICIENT READERS IN ENGLISH: SOME KEY POINTS TO REMEMBER
JO GUSMAN – WWW.NHIE.NET

Decoding Skills/Word Recognition Ideas

1. Always teach the letters and sounds of the new language within a meaningful context using culturally relevant examples and items, "being there experiences," and whole-body experiences.
2. Write what you are saying. This helps your students see the connection between oral language and the written words.
3. Use the Language Experience Approach (LEA) (Ashton-Warner, 1965). Get on your favorite search engine and type in the words "language experience approach" and download wonderful lesson plans for all grade levels and content areas.
4. Have students identify and tell you words they would like to learn how to read and write. Give them an assignment to bring "Words I Want To Learn To Read" that they see out in the "real world" such as menus, liners found on fast food restaurant trays, newspapers, signs and fliers found around their neighborhood (fliers for a garage sale, advertisements left on their door etc.).
5. Ask students to collect/record newly acquired words in a special notebook.
6. Label your classroom. You will be amazed once you start counting the hundreds of vocabulary words that surround you and your students daily!
7. Ask students to bring packaged grocery and household items from their home to use for reading lessons. Use these items for your decoding and word recognition assessments.

The English Language Learner and Language Development and Competence

1. ELLs develop language competence by using language in real, authentic communication experiences. Remember your own foreign language instruction! Did you learn more by memorizing grammar rules, or by starting with contextualized, active participation experiences? Which methods serve you best when you are in a non-English speaking country and you are trying to communicate?
2. Implement interactive and experiential learning to promote purposeful language study and use that leads to successful second language acquisition.
3. Support primary language development at school and home. Students will transfer their language competence from their first language to their new language. The bicognitive brain is amazing!
4. Incorporate the language experience approach in all grade levels.
5. Read aloud from the content area textbooks, K-12 children's literature, and other reading materials. This gives the students the opportunity to listen to the best read aloud model in the classroom, while at the same time giving them excellent examples of what the words in print should sound like. In addition, you are surrounding your students with the rhythms and patterns of the new language.

HELPING ENGLISH LANGUAGE LEARNERS BECOME PROFICIENT READERS IN ENGLISH: SOME KEY POINTS TO REMEMBER
JO GUSMAN – WWW.NHIE.NET

6. Expose your students to language that comes in the form of songs, chants, raps, rhymes, riddles, jokes, and poems. Explore and enjoy!

7. Orchestrate learning experiences in which language is greatly contextualized – orchestrate a mindful language search throughout your school building(s) and grounds, field trip sites, free community events, everyday home experiences. Collect written materials during each of these experiences and use these words for language study.

The English Language Learner and Concept/Context Building

1. Research indicates that readers are better able to understand and remember stories that reflect their cultural background (Andersson and Barnitz, 1984). Remember, all learning experiences are based on our <u>relationship</u> to the people, concepts, formats, processes, and materials we are being asked to interact with during the learning process.

2. Include narrative and expository reading materials that are culturally familiar, and provide the conceptual schemata needed to make sense out of the text the students are trying to read. Come to my website <u>www.nhie.net</u> to find the websites I recommend for you to go to and download multicultural and multilingual resources.

3. When teaching English Language Learners how to read in English, always follow the following instructional sequence -WHOLE TO PARTS never PARTS TO WHOLE. Always begin with a context-filled reading experience when using narrative or expository text, before moving into decoding text and intense language study work.

4. In order for your ELLs to learn how to read in English you must always remember **Jo Gusman's Golden Rules About Teaching ELLs How To Read In English** –

   - **The English Language Learner's English language proficiency level <u>always </u>leads the parade!"** Your student's English Language Proficiency level determines what English Language Arts/Reading Standards you will work on – Listening, Speaking, Writing, or Reading. For example, if your ELL is a Level 1, then you should select literacy strategies, processes, and skill development techniques that focus on developing their listening skills in English.
   - The best reading method to use when teaching an English Language Learner how to read in English is one that follows the **Whole to Parts instructional sequence**.
   - Our best friend when determining what reading concepts or skills to teach your English Language Learners, is to **learn more about their first language proficiency skills, specifically in listening, speaking, writing, and reading.**

HELPING ENGLISH LANGUAGE LEARNERS BECOME PROFICIENT READERS IN ENGLISH: SOME KEY POINTS TO REMEMBER
JO GUSMAN – WWW.NHIE.NET

5. Always remember – Your English Language Learners' prior knowledge holds the key to conceptual understanding. The question is, "Have you had experiences in your students' prior knowledge experiences? When we go to our students' contexts, it is only then that we learn the vocabulary, prior knowledge hooks and connections, and meaningful experiences our students use as their comprehension and understanding foundation.

Concept/Concept Building Ideas

1. Include culturally relevant narrative and expository text materials in your lessons.
2. Use instructional materials that are based on your students' familiar contexts (geographical settings, hobbies, culturally relevant activities and events).
3. Integrate stories with familiar values, lexical items, rituals and traditions.
4. Introduce unfamiliar vocabulary using whole-body, visual, and linguistic approaches. Connect the vocabulary to their world.
5. Conduct creative pre-reading discussions and activities (see my Into-Through-Beyond Literacy Framework for some practical ideas).
6. Give students the opportunity to process reading selections via read-aloud and shared reading experiences, using whole group, partner, and cooperative learning structures.
7. Always begin narrative and expository text reading experiences using "being-there"/ fieldtrip, whole body, and hands-on experiences.

The ESL Student and Critical Thinking Skills Strategies

1. It is difficult to comprehend a reading selection that is out of the realm of our own experiences, knowledge-base, or interest. Select reading materials that are high interest, gender-friendly, and culturally relevant. Look at some of the websites I recommend on my website www.nhie.net, for a variety of culturally relevant resources and materials.
2. Good readers use many reading comprehension strategies and processes. Mindfully and systematically teach, apply, and reinforce these strategies and processes using the words the students bring to you from their experiences, from their world. Remember to teach your students the processes, strategies, and skill development activities I have included in this handbook.
3. Demonstrate a variety of reading comprehension strategies to your ELLs- using highlighter pens, circling, scanning, skimming, inner speech, visualization, reading for "high visualization impact words," reading for details, etc. Teach them how to apply, what they perceive as "school only strategies" to their real world, everyday reading materials.

HELPING ENGLISH LANGUAGE LEARNERS BECOME PROFICIENT READERS IN ENGLISH: SOME KEY POINTS TO REMEMBER
JO GUSMAN – WWW.NHIE.NET

4. Give your ELLs a balanced diet of real life, high interest reading materials and isolated, skill-based reading materials. The balanced-diet literacy experience will empower your ELLs to know how to use a variety of formats and structures.

5. Help students personally and emotionally connect to narrative and expository text by using their experiences to unlock the meaning of the story or information.

6. At the beginning of the lesson, establish a personal connection and purpose for reading narrative or expository text materials. Answer the questions all readers want to know before reading something, "Why do I have to read this? When am I ever going to use this in real life" By answering these questions at the beginning of the lesson, you will help your students see the purpose and connections they need to participate in the reading experience.

7. Integrate my brain-based "Chunk-and-Chew" process throughout your direct instruction reading lessons.

8. Guide ELLs through the "story terrain." Narrative and expository text uses different story grammar frameworks. Mindfully and strategically guide your culturally and linguistically diverse students through these new frameworks, formats, and processes before they are asked to process the text on their own.

THE 4 DOORS YOUR ENGLISH LANGUAGE LEARNERS MUST GO THROUGH TO ACQUIRE ENGLISH

DOOR # 1   **DOOR # 2**   **DOOR # 3**   **DOOR # 4**

DOOR # 1_____

_____

DOOR # 2 _____

Door 1: Listening
" 2: Speaking
" 3: Writing
" 4: Reading

_____

DOOR # 3_____

_____

DOOR # 4_____

_____

THE ENGLISH LANGUAGE LEARNER'S 500 MOST IMPORTANT VOCABULARY WORDS

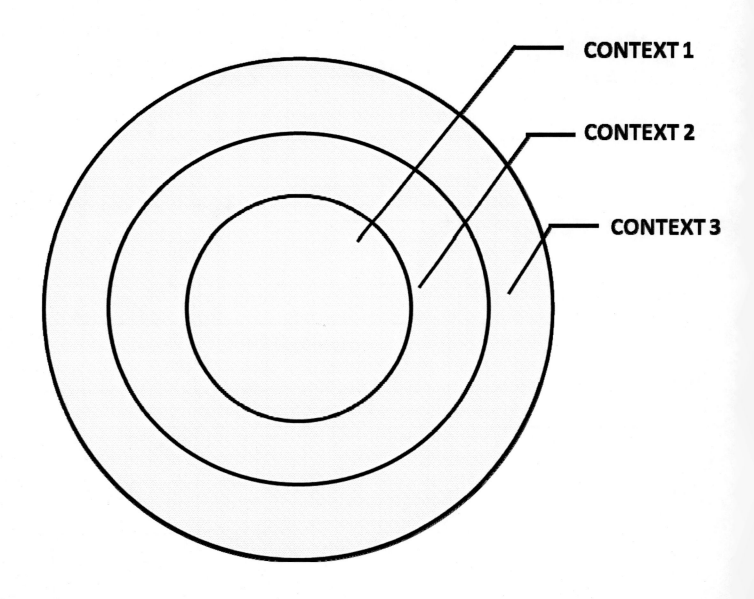

CONTEXT 1

CONTEXT 2

CONTEXT 3

THE ENGLISH LANGUAGE LEARNER'S 500 MOST IMPORTANT VOCABULARY WORDS "TO HELP MY FAMILY" CONTEXT

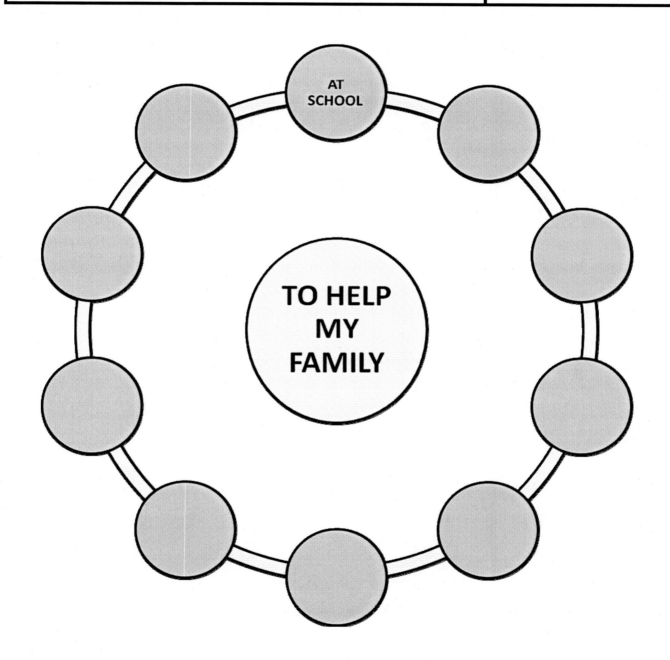

AT SCHOOL

TO HELP MY FAMILY

CAFÉ DIRECTIONS
<u>C</u>OMPLEXITY, <u>A</u>CCURACY, AND <u>F</u>LUENCY <u>E</u>VALUATION
Leal, D. J. The Word Writing CAFÉ. Reading Teacher, December/January 2005/2006

Student's Name_____ **Date:**_____

Total Words	Correct Words	1 Syllable	2 Syllables	3 Syllables	4 Syllables	5 Syllables	6 Syllables

Brain-Based Tools: Vocabulary Development

CAFÉ DIRECTIONS
COMPLEXITY, ACCURACY, AND FLUENCY EVALUATION
Leal, D. J. The Word Writing CAFÉ. Reading Teacher, December/January 2005/2006

1. Give each student several copies of the CAFÉ worksheet and 2 sharpened pencils.

2. Give the CAFÉ in a room with limited print on the walls.

3. Use the following directions. "Today I want you to write all of the English words you can in 10 minutes. Neatly write one word in each box of this worksheet. If you do not know how to spell the words, try your best, because I can't help you during this activity. Write words that tell what you like to do and where. What you can see, hear, smell, taste, or feel. Write words about your house, school, and other places you go to, or have gone to. Are there any questions? I will tell you when you have 3 minutes left.

4. Collect the CAFÉ worksheet after 10 minutes.

5. Compile and analyze the data.

6. Extension to CAFÉ Evaluation: Identify other patterns in the content and structure of the words the student wrote such as:
   a. Related words - Student writes two or more related words next to each other.
   b. Words in Categories – Student writes three or more words in a row that could be considered in a class (food, colors, sports).
   c. Complete Thoughts – Student may write phrases that relate in each box, instead of random words.
   d. Synonyms
   e. Antonyms
   f. Homonyms
   g. Nouns
   h. Adjectives
   i. Verbs
   j. Plurals
   k. Word Families
   l. Compound Words
   m. Multisyllabic Words
   n. Capitalization
   o. Combination of Parts of Speech
   p. Homophones
   q. Other

Source: Bromley, K.,Vandenberg, A., White, J. What Can We Learn From the Word Writing CAFÉ? , Reading Teacher, Vol. 61 No. 4. December 2007/January 2008 pgs. 284-295.

When I read Dr. Howard Gardner's book, *Frames Of Mind* in 1983, I realized that I had used only linguistic strategies to teach my students their spelling words. After much thought and experimentation I began to integrate different intelligences into my spelling lessons.

I orchestrated a list of strategies that would empower my students to be independent learners, problem solvers, and successful spellers. The following is my list of brain-based strategies that I taught my students, and have shared with thousands of teachers in my seminars. Teachers write me letters describing how excited their students get when it's time for Spelling! Empower your students with these retention and spelling strategies, and watch them get A's from now on.

The first time you use these strategies, create a list of <u>student generated</u> vocabulary words. The students will no doubt select personally meaningful, high interest, and culturally relevant words. By using their own words you will help your students experience immediate success.

Now teach your students to apply the following brain-based retention and spelling strategies to their own words. Once they learn how to use these strategies they will be empowered with strategies that can be applied to unfamiliar words such as content area vocabulary and other spelling words.

Before You Begin

1. Provide each student with his or her weekly spelling list, 1 index card per word on the list, an extra-large binder ring, Mr. Sketch scented markers, and 1 large 1-gallon zip-lock plastic bag (to hold their weekly spelling words).

2. Ask your students to punch a hole in the corner of <u>each</u> index card.

3. Place each index card in the binder ring.

4. Place index card ring in zip-lock bag.

MULTIPLE PATHS TO SUCCESS!
BRAIN-BASED MNEMONIC STRATEGIES
TO USE WHEN LEARNING VOCABULARY WORDS
JO GUSMAN

Preparation Time

1. Ask students to take out 1 blank index card at a time from their binder ring.
2. Tell your students that you are going to teach them some powerful brain-based spelling strategies that will help them learn how to spell each of their spelling words.
3. Model the following strategies on an overhead projector, white board, chart paper, or on actual index cards, if you are doing small group instruction.
4. Model the following strategies for about 2 weeks. Once your students learn to use each of the strategies, they will independently apply them to any list of vocabulary words you give them in the future.

Time to Teach Your Students These Powerful Brain-Based Mnemonic Strategies

1. **Pen Talk Echo-Chant**
   Students follow teacher's visual directions on how to properly write each spelling word. Students write each spelling word in a different color. Ask students to echo chant the spelling of each letter as they write the word. Giving each word a rhythmic association helps your students integrate the musical intelligence into their learning process. This will help them retain the word in their long-term memory.

   | ○ | **cat** |

2. **Configuration**
   Using a different color for each word, ask students to outline each of their spelling words. Giving each word a colored shape will help your students <u>visualize</u> a shape and word.

   | ○ | **cat** |

3. **Spatial Definition**
   Ask students to turn their spelling card over to the blank side. Read the definition of the spelling word from a dictionary. Now, ask your students to draw their definition of the spelling word based on what that word means in their own home, neighborhood, culture, or any other personal experiences. This helps your students give each word a culturally relevant definition that they won't forget!

4. Sensory Integration-Skin Memory

The largest organ in the human body is our skin! Let's teach the kids how to use their skin to help them remember how to spelling each word.

Self Practice -Ask students to roll up their sleeves. Using their pointer finger, ask them to write one spelling word at a time on their inner arm. Students will see the spelling word on their own inner arm.

Partner Practice – Students practice writing one word at a time on each other's inner arm. Because of the tickling sensation the students will feel, they will close their eyes, and now you will see the word in your head. Hurray, you just led students to the most powerful spelling strategy of all – VISUALIZE YOUR WORDS!

5. Visualize and Store

Teach students to study their words by looking at the color, shape, and number of letters in each word. Now, teach them to use their "photographic memory" and take a picture of each of their spelling words, and store it in their memory bank. Tell them that this technique will help them visualize the word that you call out during Friday's spelling test.

6. Spatial Grounding

This is one of my favorite mnemonic strategies that I teach students! Write each spelling word on a large sheet of white construction paper. Write each word in a different color and give each word a different colored shape. Select a location in your classroom to teach the spelling word. This strategy helps the student place the spelling word in their "spatial memory," thus creating a spatial/location association for each spelling word. Students will remember where you were standing, and where you placed the word. On the day of the spelling test, ask your students to simply look at the location where you "parked the word," visualize the word in that location, and then write the word on their test page.

7. Meta-Talk Time (Share Your Metacognition)

Ask students to think about the different strategies they have created to help them study their spelling words. Have students show their classmates how to use these strategies. Students feel so proud when they teach their fellow classmates new strategies to add on to their word study repertoire.

8. **Independent Practice**

Use some of the following vocabulary builder practice worksheets to help your students practice their spelling words at home. You will find different formats of these practice pages.

Enjoy teaching and empowering your students with these powerful brain-based strategies! Now, just sit back and see your students smile when they get that big A+ on their spelling test.

Jo Gusman

Vocabulary Builder

Write your vocabulary word 3 times in your best handwriting.

1. _____
2. _____
3. _____

Write the definition of this word

Draw a picture of your definition

Use the word in 2-3 sentences

THE TRANSFER BRIDGE

VOCABULARY WORD	DRAW A PICTURE OF WHAT THIS WORD MEANS TO YOU
1.	
2.	
3.	
4.	

Brain-Based Tools: Vocabulary Development

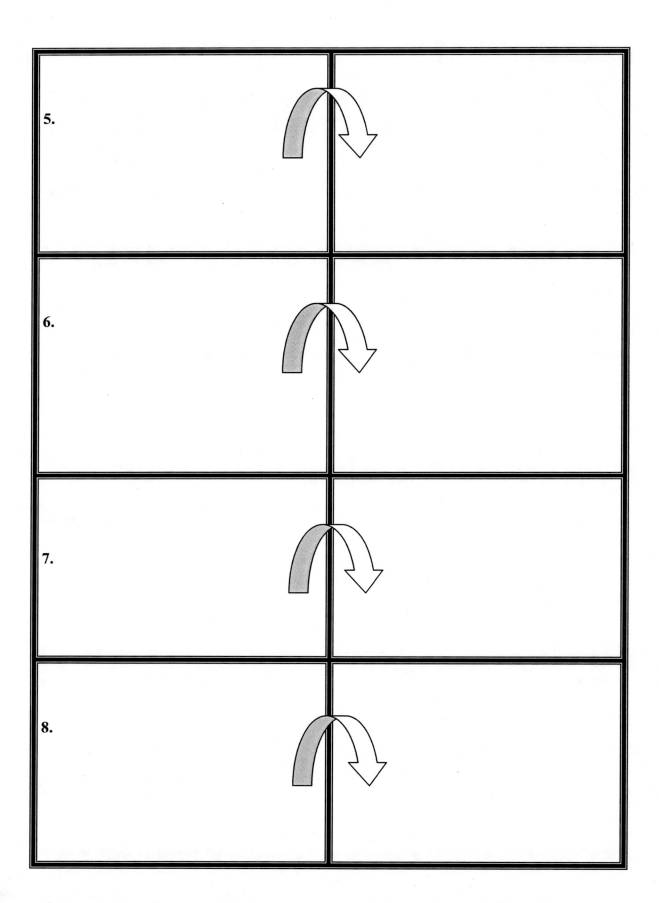

PERSONAL CHARACTERISTICS VOCABULARY BUILDING

1. DEVELOPS THE STUDENT'S TEXT-TO-SELF RELATIONSHIP.

2. STUDENTS USE THEIR OWN INTEREST AND PRIOR KNOWLEDGE TO ENHANCE VOCABULARY GROWTH.

3. STUDENTS GENERATE VOCABULARY WORDS TO BE EXPLORED AND LEARNED.

Personal characteristics vocabulary building graphic organizer and the bilingual student: _____

_____

_____

_____

_____

_____

_____

_____

_____

_____

PERSONAL CHARACTERISTICS VOCABULARY BUILDING

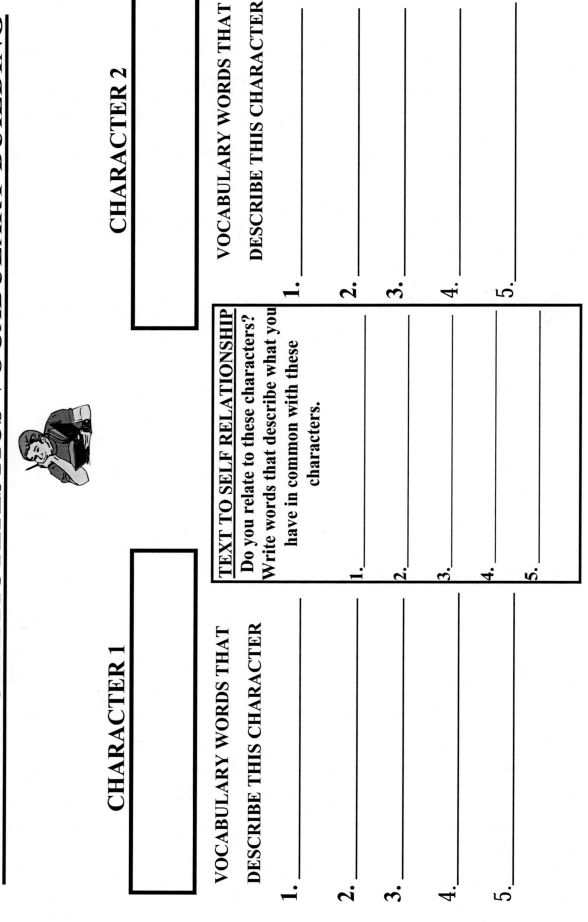

CHARACTER 2

VOCABULARY WORDS THAT
DESCRIBE THIS CHARACTER

1. _____

2. _____

3. _____

4. _____

5. _____

TEXT TO SELF RELATIONSHIP
Do you relate to these characters?
Write words that describe what you
have in common with these
characters.

1. _____

2. _____

3. _____

4. _____

5. _____

CHARACTER 1

VOCABULARY WORDS THAT
DESCRIBE THIS CHARACTER

1. _____

2. _____

3. _____

4. _____

5. _____

PROCESSING TEXT
PRACTICAL IDEAS

Do you use highlighter pens to help you process text you are reading? Do you write notes in the margin, circle or underline words? Share these powerful processing strategies with your English Language Learners.

Teach your students how to use highlighter pens and Post-It flags to identify main ideas, specific words, or punctuation marks.

Make a copy of specific pages from your content area textbook or basal reader. Students are now free to circle, underline, highlight, and write notes in the margin, translate, and freely interact with the text they are reading.

POST-IT MARGIN CODES

Empower your students with Post-It Margin Codes. Students use their Post-It Margin Codes to immediately respond to the text they are reading. When they find a word, sentence, or paragraph they do not understand, want more information about, or are excited to share with you, they simply put one of their Post-It Margin Code tags on the margin. This holds their thought, until you are able to come and work with them individually.

DIRECTIONS:

1. Give students several 5 X 3 Post-It Sheets.
2. Students cut their Post-Its into strips.
3. They draw the symbol and words for each Post-It Margin Code on each strip.
4. Place each type of Post-It Margin Code strip into stacks.
5. Put Post-It Margin Code strips in textbooks ready to be used in the next lesson.

EXAMPLES:

HURRAY! I KNOW THIS! ☆	THIS IS NEW INFORMATION
I HAVE A QUESTION	WOW! THIS IS EXCITING!

WORD SPLASH
PRE-READING ACTIVITY

1. Make an overhead transparency of page 65.

2. Ask students to open their basal readers or content area textbooks, to the chapter that will be read that week.

3. Give students time to look at all of the illustrations, diagrams, and words in the chapter.

4. Ask students to point to a word they do not know how to read, or know its meaning.

5. Write the words that each student shows you on the Word Splash overhead transparency.

6. Point to, and read each word on the overhead to your students. Define the word verbally, visually, and by acting out the word meaning.

7. Ask students to chant each word with you.

8. Ask each student to select a word on the Word Splash overhead transparency to read aloud and define.

WORD SPLASH

K What do you know?	**W** What do you want to know?	**L** What have you learned?	**R** What further research would you like to do?

LOOK AT MY THOUGHTS

WRITE A QUOTE YOU FOUND IMPORTANT FROM THIS PARAGRAPH	DRAW OR WRITE YOUR THOUGHTS ABOUT THIS QUOTE
PARAGRAPH #____	
PARAGRAPH #____	
PARAGRAPH #____	
PARAGRAPH #____	

ANTICIPATION-REACTION GUIDE

Research-Base: Content-Area Reading: An Integrated Approach. Readence, Bean and Baldwin. 1981, 1985, 1989. Dubuque, IA: Kendall/Hunt.

1. Activates student's knowledge about a topic before reading the text.

2. Pre and post reading strategy.

3. A graphic guide to help build student's comprehension by asking them to react to a series of statements before they begin to read the text.

   Anticipation-Reaction guide and the bilingual student _____

   _____

   _____

   _____

ANTICIPATION/REACTION GUIDE

AGREE	DISAGREE	STATEMENTS	AGREE	DISAGREE
		1.		
		2.		
		3.		
		4.		
		5.		

Brain-Based Tools: Comprehension

ANTICIPATION-REACTION GUIDE

A great graphic organizer to help your students examine attitudes before and after listening to or reading a story.

DIRECTIONS:

1. Teacher selects statements from the selection students are about to listen to or read.

2. Teacher reads aloud selected statements to students. Using their anticipation-reaction guide, ask students to respond to the statement by checking off the AGREE or DISAGREE box.

3. AFTER students have listened to or read the selection, ask to students to revisit their response by checking off the AGREE or DISAGREE box.

4. Ask students to discuss and process any changes in their opinions.

SEMANTIC FEATURE ANALYSIS

Research-Base: Johnson, D. D., and P. D. Pearson. 1978. Teaching Reading Vocabulary. New York: Hold, Rinehart & Winston.

1. Designed to help students improve comprehension and vocabulary and categorization skills.

2. Helps students understand the similarities and differences in related words.

3. Strategy helps students expand and retain content area vocabulary and concepts.

Semantic feature analysis and the bilingual student

_____

_____

_____

_____

_____

Brain-Based Tools - Comprehension

SEMANTIC FEATURE ANALYSIS

A great graphic organizer and strategy to help your students develop their comprehension, vocabulary,and categorization skills. Can also be used to refine and reinforce vocabulary and related concepts in a post-reading of content area textbook materials. Johnson and Pearson (1978) recommend the following six steps;

<u>Directions:</u>

1. <u>CATEGORY SELECTION</u> -Teacher selects a category (e.g. pets, types of governments) related to a topics the class is studying. Record on feature analysis matrix.

2. <u>LIST WORDS IN CATEGORY</u> - Teacher lists words in selected category that name concepts or objects related to selected category. When students become familiar with the strategy, they should provide the words. Record on feature analysis matrix.

3. <u>LIST FEATURES</u> —Teacher identifies traits to explore in the selected category. Record on feature analysis matrix.

4. <u>INDICATE FEATURE POSSESSION</u> -Teacher guides students through the feature matrix. Use a simple +/- system to indicate feature possession.

5. **<u>ADD WORDS/FEATURES</u>** – Teacher or students generate new words to be added to feature analysis matrix, followed by new features to be analyzed.

6. **<u>COMPLETE AND EXPLORE MATRIX</u>** – Students complete the feature analysis matrix. Students examine how words in the matrix relate – noting similarities and differences.

SEMANTIC FEATURE ANALYSIS CHART

TOPIC: →	TRAIT	TRAIT	TRAIT	TRAIT
1.				
2.				
3.				
4.				

79   Brain-Based Tools: Comprehension

MOVIE TIME READ ALOUD
Jo Gusman

1. Teacher reads aloud to student(s)

2. Student(s) visualize passage teacher is reading

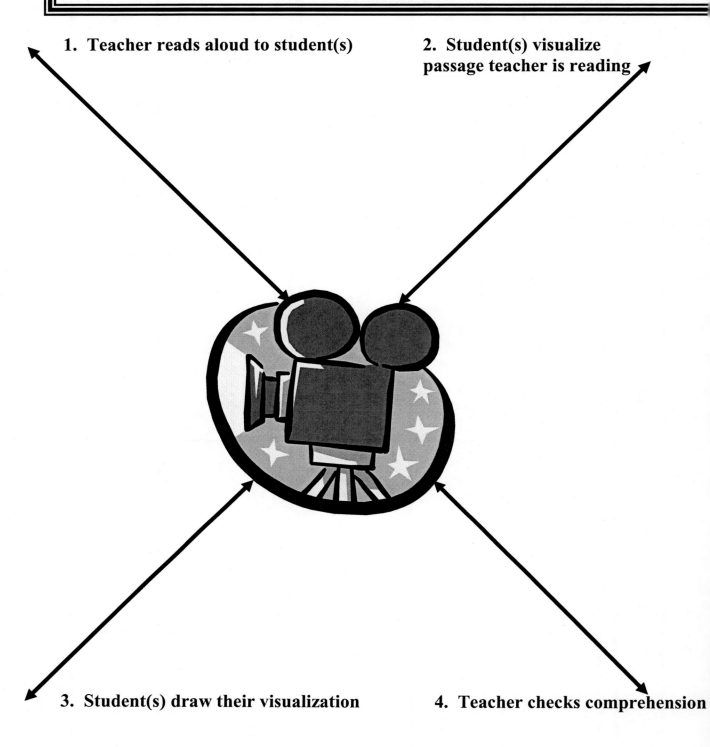

3. Student(s) draw their visualization

4. Teacher checks comprehension

80   Brain-Based Tools: Comprehension

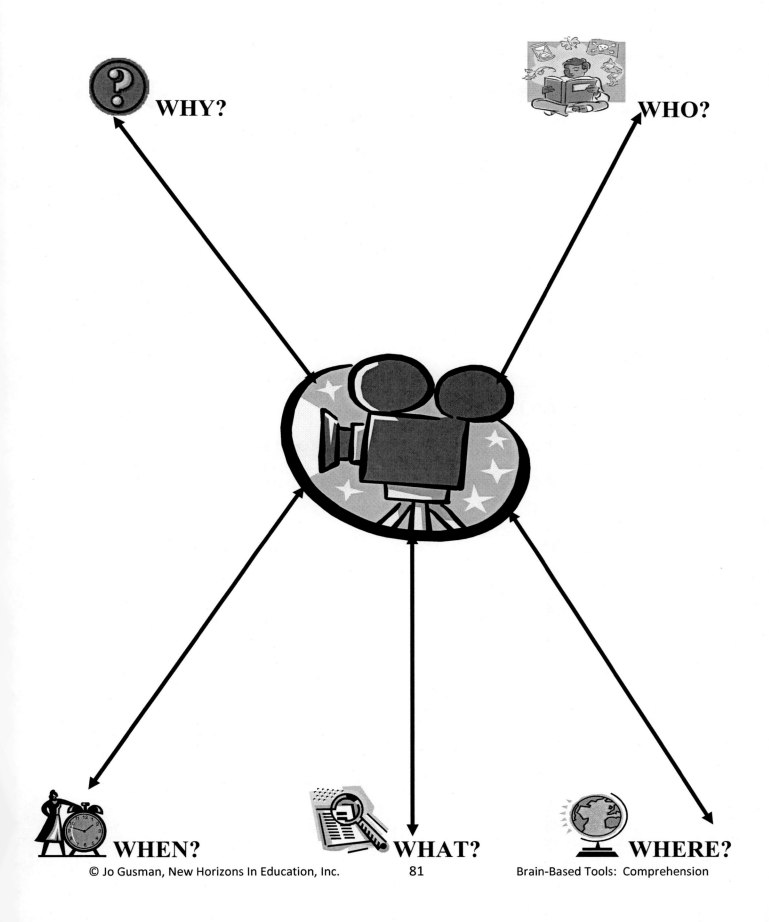

WHY?

WHO?

WHEN?

WHAT?

WHERE?

READ AND VISUALIZE TELL BACK PROCESS

A great reading process to help your students develop their visualization, reading comprehension, re-telling, and active listening skills.

<u>Directions:</u>

1. Students work with their Language Buddy. (ESL or primary language buddy)

2. Students are assigned or select the Movie Maker (visualizer) or Reader role.

3. Reader reads a paragraph or more from a story.

4. Movie Maker creates a mental picture of the words being read.

5. Movie Maker tells Reader words, phrases, or sentences that describe their mental movie.

6. Students now compare the Movie Maker's images to the illustrations in the book.

7. Students switch roles.

<u>Extension:</u> Students can draw their images. Drawings can then be used as springboards for a Language Experience story.

WHAT'S ON YOUR MIND?

DIRECTIONS: Draw your thoughts about the story you are reading. Write any questions you have about the story.

83

Brain-Based Tools: Comprehension

FACT-FEELING FLIP BOOK

1.

Stack 3 sheets of of white paper.

2.

Fold paper to create a book.

3.

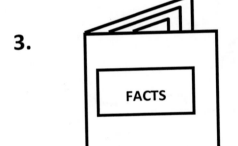

FACTS

Write the word "FACTS" on the cover of the book.

4.

FEELINGS

Flip the book over. Write the word "FEELINGS" on the new blank cover.

DIRECTIONS: Use the FACT-FEELING flip book during directed instruction or while reading a content area textbook. Draw or write the important facts you read. Draw or write your feelings about the information you are reading.

JO'S NOTE TAKING AND PROCESSING TEXT IDEAS

Help your English Language Learners process your verbal directed instruction lessons by inviting them to take notes as you speak. Have them take notes in the following ways:

 DRAW

 **COPY**

 WRITE IN THEIR PRIMARY LANGUAGE

 WRITE IN ENGLISH

 **DOODLE**

JO'S NOTE TAKING AND PROCESSING TEXT GRAPHIC ORGANIZERS

On the following pages, you will find some note taking templates that I designed to help English Language Learners process highly linguistic information during directed instruction, or as they read, process, and try to comprehend content area textbooks. To guarantee that your students successfully use these note taking graphic organizers, model and use role-play to demonstrate the proper use of these templates.

1. **PARAGRAPH DRAW**

2. **LEARNING QUILT**

3. **SENSES PROCESSING CHART**

4. **CAUSE AND EFFECT FISHBONE WEB**

5. **STORY STAR**

PARAGRAPH DRAW

PARAGRAPH #_____	**PARAGRAPH #_____**	**PARAGRAPH #_____**
PARAGRAPH #_____	**PARAGRAPH #_____**	**PARAGRAPH #_____**

PARAGRAPH DRAW

Our English Language Learners many times are not able to read the English language, but they understand when it is read aloud to them. Use this pre-reading process to help your students comprehend a story or chapter in a content-area textbook.

1. Give each student the Paragraph Draw worksheet.

2. Teacher reads aloud one paragraph at a time while students actively listen and visualize.

3. Students write the number of the paragraph the teacher is reading aloud in each box of their Paragraph Draw worksheet.

4. Students draw a picture of the main idea(s) for each paragraph in the corresponding boxes. Teacher checks the students' drawings to make sure they correspond with main idea read aloud.

PARAGRAPH #_____

PARAGRAPH #_____

PARAGRAPH #_____

PARAGRAPH #_____

PARAGRAPH #_____

PARAGRAPH #_____

THE LEARNING QUILT

Use a language signal and the Learning Quilt graphic organizer to help you make your directed instruction more comprehensible. A language signal is a verbal signal you use consistently that alerts your students that important information is about to be delivered verbally by you. Students record the key point you delivered verbally onto their Learning Quilt graphic organizer. By using these two strategies and processes, you will make your input more comprehensible during content area lessons.

1. Give each student a copy of the Learning Quilt graphic organizer.

2. Make an overhead transparency of the Learning Quilt. Place the transparency on your overhead projector. Use Vis-à-Vis pens to write each key point on the Learning Quilt transparency.

3. Integrate a language signal into your directed instruction process.

4. Verbally present a "key point". Now, write and draw 1 key point per box on the Learning Quilt transparency. Students copy the key point onto their Learning Quilt.

5. Remember - Write only 1 key point in each box. Use words and pictures to describe your key point. Write each key point using a different color Vis-à-Vis pen. Use different colors to help your students visualize and remember the key points you presented.

LEARNING QUILT

1.	2.
3.	4.
5.	6.
7.	8.

SENSES PROCESSING CHART

DIRECTIONS: Teach students to use their senses to help them comprehend a story or content area information they are reading. Ask students to draw pictures and write words that describe the story they are reading.

DESCRIBE WHAT YOU SEE	DESCRIBE WHAT YOU HEAR	DESCRIBE WHAT YOU FEEL	DESCRIBE WHAT YOU SMELL	DESCRIBE WHAT YOU TASTE

92   Brain-Based Tools: Comprehension

DESCRIBE WHAT YOU SEE	DESCRIBE WHAT YOU HEAR	DESCRIBE WHAT YOU FEEL	DESCRIBE WHAT YOU SMELL	DESCRIBE WHAT YOU TASTE

93

Brain-Based Tools: Comprehension

CAUSE-EFFECT GRAPHIC ORGANIZER

THE EFFECT:

THE CIVIL WAR

1. Write 1 event that led to the Civil War.

2. Write 1 event that led to the Civil War.

3. Write 1 event that led to the Civil War.

4. Write 1 event that led to the Civil war.

5. Write 1 event that led to the Civil War.

6. Write 1 event that led to the Civil War.

DIRECTIONS: 1. Make an overhead transparency or draw this graphic organizer on the board.
2. Give each student a copy of the cause and effect graphic organizer.
3. Write and draw "the target" for the lesson inside of the effect box.
4. Through the directed instruction process, write the events that led to the Civil War on each "cause arrow."
5. Students follow along as you present your lesson using this graphic organizer.

©Jo Gusman, New Horizons In Education, Inc.

94

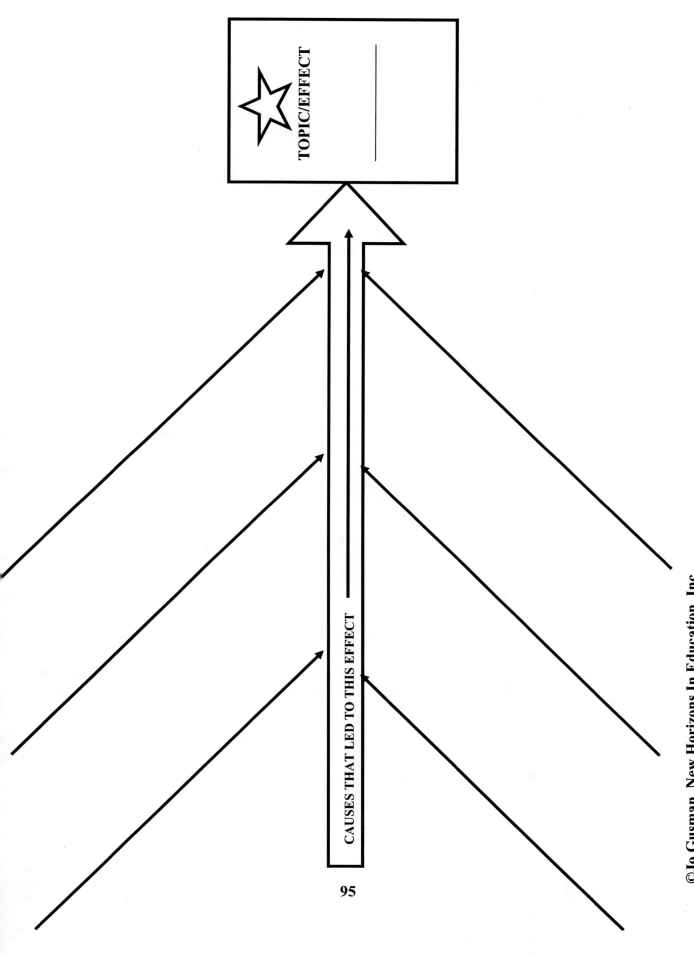

TOPIC/EFFECT

CAUSES THAT LED TO THIS EFFECT

95

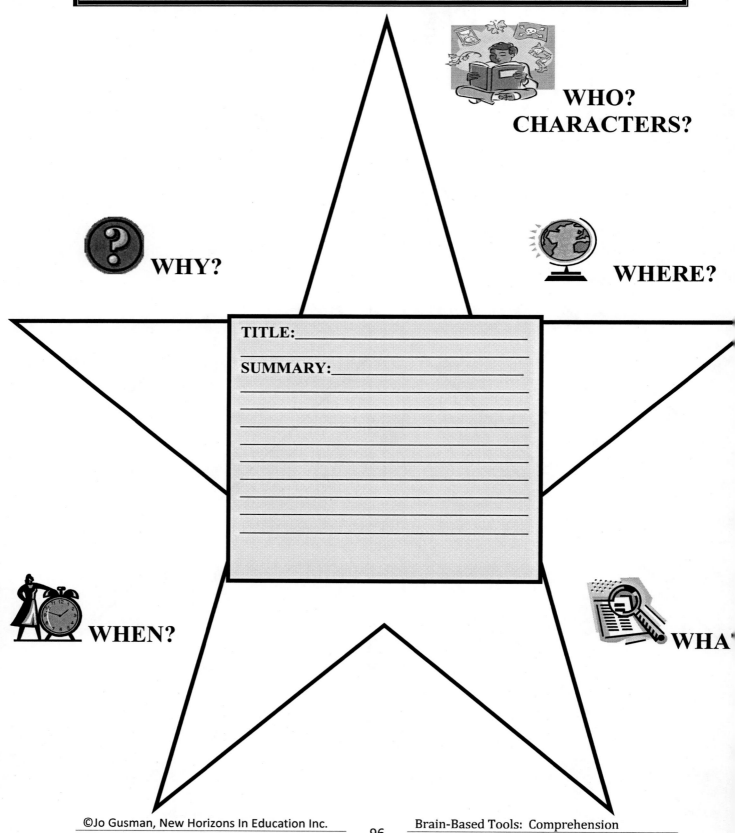

Brain-Based Tools: Comprehension

THE ABC'S OF IT ALL
A CHECKING FOR UNDERSTANDING GAME

I developed this game after I saw how frustrated English Language Learners became when I would ask comprehension questions in English. They understood the concepts I was teaching, but did not feel confident enough to verbalize their answers. To participate in this game, ELL and English speakers need only give 1-word responses or point to the word they want to say. This process allows <u>everyone</u> to participate, and lets you assess your students' comprehension of the concept you are teaching.

Directions:

1. Make several overhead transparencies of the *ABC'S of It All* game board on page 98. Keep them near your ELMO/overhead projector.
2. Place the *ABC's of It All* transparency on your projector. Write the topic you will be teaching in the topic circle.
3. Tell your students that you will be checking for understanding throughout your lesson – approximately every 11-17 minutes.
4. When you are ready to check for understanding, say the following to your students:

    * *"Tell yourself 1 word you now know about_____."*

    * *"Write the word on a piece of paper."*
      (Remind the students that the words can be found in their textbook, journal, word wall, etc.)

    * *"Circle the first letter of your word."*

    * *"If you want to play the game, raise your hand. When I see your hand up, I will point to you. When I point to you, tell me the first letter of your word. I will write your word in that letter box."*

5. To win the game, every one of the letter boxes must be filled in with information about the topic you are teaching. (You may have to give the X, Y, and Z boxes as free spots, if there are no words beginning with those letters.)
6. Have a great time!

THE ABC'S OF IT ALL

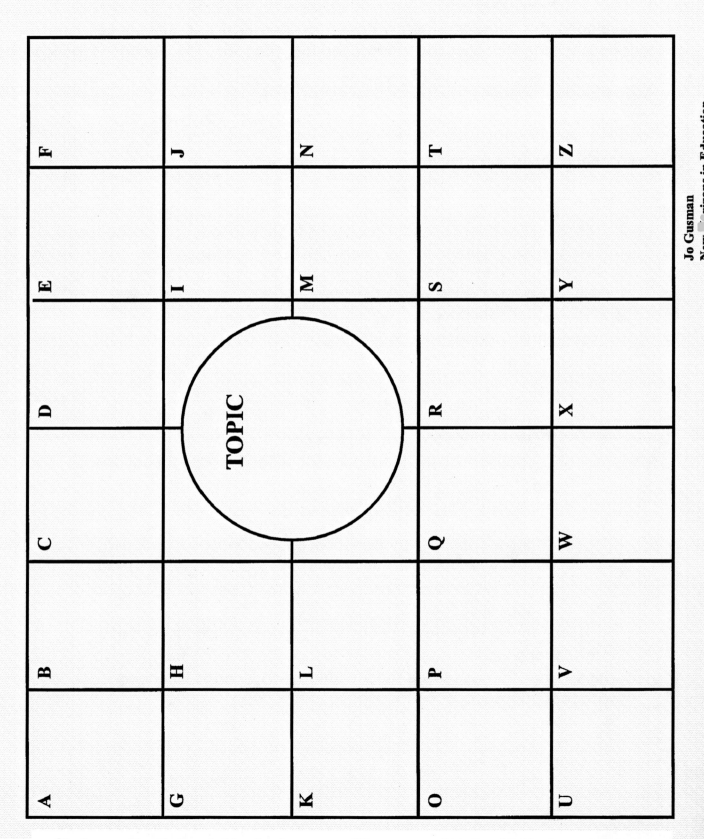

 Brain-Based Tools: Comprehension

DEFINE FLUENCY: _____

_____

_____

_____

BRAIN-BASED DEFINITION: _____

_____

_____

_____

THE BIG V AND FLUENCY: _____

_____

_____

_____

THE 2 *Ms*:

M _____

M _____

A SCHOLAR'S WALK

I developed this fluency process after observing several professors walking, talking, and reading what appeared to be research papers to fellow colleagues. I began to wonder if I could improve fluency by having my students process text while walking during the read aloud process. I experimented with the idea and started to call this read aloud process, A Scholar's Walk. I was amazed at the results.

Brain research to support this activity can be found in Dr. Carla Hannaford's book, **Smart Moves**, and **Brain Gym**, by Drs. Paul and Gail Dennison.

Directions:

1. Ask each student to bring a book to the Scholar's Walk area (classroom, hallway, outdoors).

2. Students stand in a line behind the teacher.

3. Ask students to open their basal readers or content area textbooks, to the chapter that will be read aloud.

4. Give students time to look at all of the illustrations, diagrams, and words in the chapter.

5. Teacher walks slowly while reading aloud to the students. Students read along while following the teacher.

6. Teacher and students stop walking. Teacher identifies key vocabulary words in passage read aloud. Teacher asks students to define the word verbally and by acting out the word meaning.

7. Teacher asks students to chant each word.

8. Teacher continues the Scholar's Walk. Teacher asks for volunteers to read aloud the next paragraphs. Continue process until entire passage has been read aloud and processed.

TIPS FOR IMPROVING ORAL READING FLUENCY

Read the latest brain research on the effects of movement on language and literacy.

Recommended Books

1. *Brain Gym*. Drs. Gail and Paul Dennison
2. *Smart Moves*. Dr. Carla Hannaford

Practical Brain-Based Fluency Ideas

1. Expose your students to the best read-aloud models in your classroom, school, and community. Surround the students with outstanding read-aloud models who can effectively model creative expression, rate, flow, and the melodic rhythm of language.
2. Unison Reading
3. Partner Reading
4. Repeated Readings
5. Recorded books so your students can read along while listening.
6. Read aloud multicultural poetry
7. Readers Theater and plays – This is a great way to practice fluency and dramatic expression.
8. Read aloud and allow them to feel the rhythmic patterns and flow of their new language. Remember, every language has its own beat, rhythm and volume.

ELA AND ELD

ELA/READING	ELD

Handwritten note:

Too many variables.
Are you willing to 1)
identify all the variables
and 2) assess all the
variables and 3) create
a program based on
the variables?
*Answer to comparing 2 ELLs.

ELA and ELD: What I plan to ~~do with this~~ information

PREVIEW → REVIEW
INSTRUCTIONAL PROCESS
FOR THE MAINSTREAM CLASSROOM

"The conceptual load of new content is intensified for ESL students by their lack of familiarity with the language. It is exacerbated by the linguistic complexity of accompanying text, which is most often written for native English speakers. The immediate goal of the teacher is to make content comprehensible" (Krashen & Terrell, 1983).

As a Bilingual Education instructional assistant and Bilingual Education teacher in a multilingual classroom, I found this instructional process to be highly effective when teaching content area lessons. Preview-Review is a process that gives the English Language Learner advanced prior knowledge about the forthcoming lesson to be presented to the entire class in English.

In its original form, the Preview-Review method is defined as, "a bilingual instructional approach in which content areas are previewed in one language, presented in the other and reviewed in the first" (Lessow-Hurley, 1990). The bilingual teacher would follow the following steps:

1. Preview – An introduction and explanation of the concepts, skills, main ideas, key vocabulary are presented in the primary language (L1). This step could be seen as the anticipatory set in the student's first language. The Preview should take approximately 10-15+ minutes.

2. Mini Lesson – The body of the content area lesson is now presented in "comprehensible input" English.

3.   **Review** – Check for understanding in the primary language. Use cooperative learning structures where students who speak the same language can now process the mini-lesson content, ask questions for clarification, and share their understanding of the key concepts in the lesson. Allocate 5-15 minutes for this part of the lesson.

I found the need to modify the Preview-Review process when I found myself as a Spanish-English Bilingual teacher at a Newcomer school classroom where my students spoke Hmong, Mien, Lao, Vietnamese and variety of other languages and dialects that I did not speak. My charge was to teach them how to speak English and to teach them content area concepts and skills. This is truly a challenge when you cannot speak their language.   The following is a description of how I modified this very powerful instructional process that was originally intended for a Bilingual Education classroom.   During the Preview you or your Preview-Review Teaching Partner (bilingual instructional assistant or bilingual student) provide a Preview of the conceptual focus of the lesson, skills, all visuals and graphic organizers, and instructional formats used in the textbook in the student's primary language (L1).

PREVIEW ➡ REVIEW
INSTRUCTIONAL PROCESS FOR THE MAINSTREAM CLASSROOM

1. PREVIEW

1. Teacher presents content area lesson in the student's primary language.

OR

2. Teacher asks bilingual students or instructional assistant to be their Preview-Review Teaching Partner (PRTP). Teacher provides the Preview-Review Teaching Partners an overview of the concepts, skills, vocabulary, activities, graphic organizers, etc. the English Language Learner will encounter. The content area lesson will then be presented the next day or week. The next day or week the Preview-Review Teaching Partner provides the preview of the content area lesson in the student's primary language.

OR

3. On the first day of the content area lesson, the teacher presents the content area concepts in a visual/spatial form, such as a movie, instead of relying on English verbal and written input.

2. REVIEW

1. **Mini Lesson Version: Teacher presents the content area lesson in English using visuals, hands-on, whole body, and linguistic materials that provide the English Language Learners with a "comprehensible input" lesson. The students will comprehend the lesson in English because you have already provided them with a preview of the concepts,skills, vocabulary etc. in their own language.**

OR

2. **Check for understanding in the primary language. Use cooperative learning structures which encourage students who speak the same language to process the mini-lesson content, ask questions for clarification, and share their understanding of the key concepts in the lesson. Allocate 5-15 minutes for this part of the lesson.**

CHUNK-N-CHEW
JO GUSMAN'S
DIRECTED INSTRUCTION PROCESS

It's all about timing! In 1983, I realized that I sounded like Charlie Brown's teacher, when I spoke only English to my ELL students. I became aware of the overwhelmed look on their faces when I taught highly conceptual content area lessons in English. To make matters worse, if my directed instruction lesson went on too long, I would completely lose my student's attention.

During this time period, I was attending brain-based education seminars. I learned that the brain could only process auditory information for approximately 11-17 minute cycles. I integrated this brain research into a directed instruction process I started calling, "Chunk-n-Chew." The Chunk-n-Chew process provides you with an optimum teaching rhythm that will help your ESL students listen, process, and understand your directed instruction lessons in English.

CHUNK-N-CHEW
DIRECTED INSTRUCTION PROCESS

CHUNK

Teacher presents lesson in 11-17 minute chunks.

Make your input more comprehensible by using the Multiple Intelligences. Use a variety of intelligences such as bodily-kinesthetic, musical, spatial.

CHEW

Give students 5-15 minutes to process your chunk.

Students can process your chunk in the following ways:

1. <u>Intrapersonal/Reflection Time</u>- Students draw, write in their journal, reflect, talk to themselves in their own language, or silently re-read notes or other written materials.

2. <u>L^1 or L^2 Partners</u> – Partners review and re-teach your chunk with a partner in their primary language or in English.

3. <u>Cooperative Learning Group</u> – Using cooperative learning structures, have students process the chunk you taught.

4. <u>Whole Class</u> – Use guided practice techniques to help students complete a section of a worksheet, or answer questions at the end of the chapter.

RECOMMENDED PRACTICES FOR TEACHING CONTENT AREA LESSONS TO ENGLISH LANGUAGE LEARNERS CHECKLIST

Adapted from: Content Area Literacy: An Integrated Approach. John Readence, W. Bean, R. Scott Baldwin. Kendall/Hunt Publishing Company, 2000

Check the appropriate number showing how much you do each of these.
1. **Almost always**
2. **Most of the time**
3. **Sometimes**
4. **Seldom**
5. **Never**

	1	2	3	4	5
1. The teacher utilizes all language processes (listening, speaking, writing, and reading) to enhance students' learning with text.					
2. The second language acquisition and reading levels of the students are known by the teacher.					
3. Lesson planning structures/formats use the students' cultural backgrounds as a foundation for the content area lesson.					
4. The teacher has pre-read the written material to evaluate the text for the presence or absence of characteristics which make a well-organized text for English Language Learners.					
5. Materials for the content area lesson are chosen to match the second language acquisition and reading levels of the students.					
6. Books and other instructional materials are available for students who read below and above the readability level of the text.					
7. Textbook aids, such as illustrations, maps, and graphic organizers are explained or called to the attention of the students.					
8. A portion of the Pre-Reading time is spent on discussing how to read the text effectively.					
9. The teacher presents the specialized vocabulary and concepts in the context of a well-planned lesson and directed instruction time. (i.e. during Preview-Review lesson delivery process)					

10. Prior knowledge of the concepts and text concepts are activated before reading the text.					
11. Purpose is stated for each reading assignment. Teacher connects the purpose to the English Language Learner's role in their family. Stated purpose answers student's question: "Why do we have to learn this?"					
12. Assignments are clearly and concisely explained using visuals, demonstrations, modeling, and words that are comprehensible to the English Language Learner's language level.					
13. The teacher adapts instruction and materials to the ability and language level of students.					
14. The teacher asks questions designed to promote thinking at all levels of comprehension.					
15. The teacher provides some form of study guide, listening guide, or outline to aid in the comprehension of the text and verbal instruction.					
16. The course content includes reading more than a single textbook. A variety of supplemental textbooks and materials are included in the instructional process.					
17. A variety of "comprehensible input" reference materials, software, and audio-visuals are made available to the teacher and students during the directed instruction.					
18. Students are taught how to locate and use a variety of reference materials.					
19. Students are encouraged to read a wide variety of materials and genres related to the textbook lesson.					
20. Directed, whole group, cooperative learning, small group, and individual instruction is used during the instructional process.					
21. Cooperative learning – Dr. Spencer Kagan's The Structural Approach – is used during the instructional process to promote comprehension and insure comprehensible input.					
22. Native language is used to help students comprehend concepts, skills, process, and procedures.					

HOW TO READ A TEXTBOOK

The format of a textbook affects the reading strategies a student uses. The more organizational and formatting aids there are, the easier it is for students to make sense of the materials. Students can benefit from direct instruction in how to use the following:

☐ Cover

☐ Table of Contents

☐ Index

☐ Preface and/or introduction

☐ Conclusion or summary

☐ Pictures, graphs, tables, figures (Images contain much more information than straight text)

☐ Section Headings (These help the reader understand the book's structure)

☐ Special typeface or formatting: boldface, italics, numbered items, lists

☐ Questions

☐ Vocabulary lists

Source: Literacy Matters website

WEBSITES THAT OFFER SPECIFIC STRATEGIES TO HELP STUDENTS LEARN HOW TO READ TEXTBOOKS

English Across the Curriculum: Language Demands of a Textbook
www.english.unitecnology.ac.nz/resources/resources/learntolearn/demands.html

Improving Students' Understanding of Textbook Content
www.ldonline.org/ld_indepth/teaching_techniques/understanding_textbooks.html

Ways of Reading Text
http://slc.otago.ac.nz/studyskills/ch3sect2.asp

Study Skills for Middle School: Reading Tips! SQ3R
www.fm.cnyric.org/eagle_Hill/bowers/read.htm

Textbook Organization
http://muskingum.edu/~cal/database/general/reading.html

Textbook literacy and my ELLs _____

_____

_____

_____

_____

_____

TEXTBOOK QUESTION AND ANSWER ORGANIZER

QUESTION	ANSWER AND PAGE #
1.	PAGE # ___
2.	PAGE # ___
3.	PAGE # ___
4.	PAGE # ___
5.	PAGE # ___

PAGE # _____

PAGE # _____

PAGE # _____

PAGE # _____

PAGE # _____

6.

7.

8.

9.

10.

BRAIN-BASED WRITING PROCESS

1. **Sensory-Filled Being-There Experience**
   Orchestrate a multisensory "being-there" experience for your students (i.e. cook, take a walk, do a hands-on activity, go on a field trip).

2. **Visualize**
   Ask students to recall and visualize the "being there" experience through a guided visualization.

3. **Draw or Create A 3D Project**
   Students draw their visualization on a long sheet of white construction paper, or by creating a diorama or other 3D project.

4. **Listening and Speaking Time**
   With a partner, students take turns describing their drawing or project . Students can describe their drawing or project in L1 or L1.

5. **Writing Process**
   Using their art project as a springboard, guide students through the Writing Process.

6. **Reading**
   Students share their stories in large or small groups.

SENSORY MIND MAP

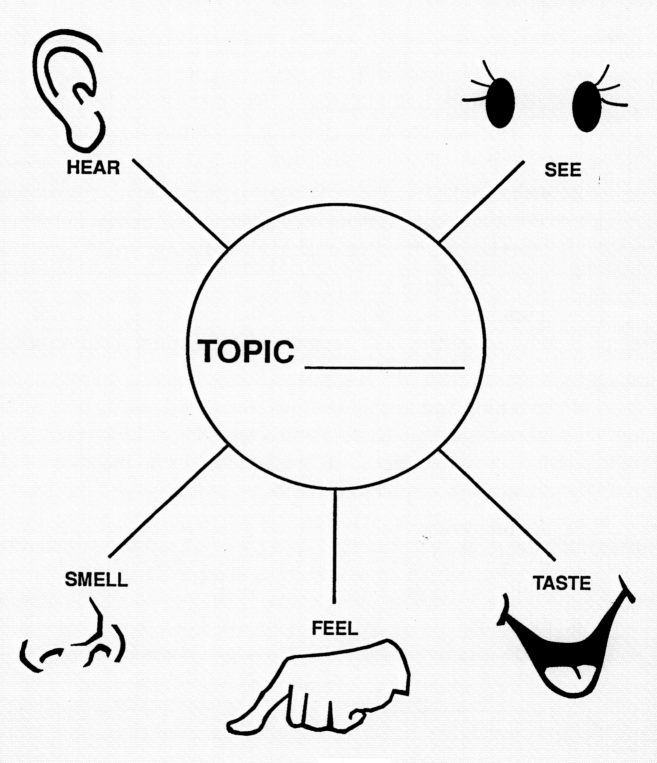

TOPIC _____

HEAR

SEE

SMELL

FEEL

TASTE

117

MIX-AND-MATCH STORYMAKER

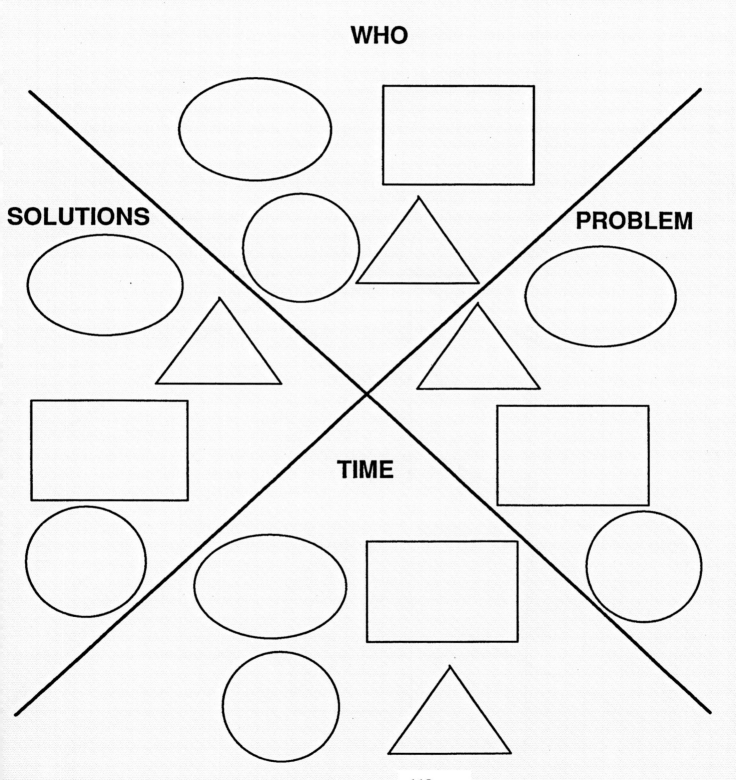

WHO

SOLUTIONS

PROBLEM

TIME

118

STORY SUMMARY FISHBONE GRAPHIC ORGANIZER

SUMMARY:

WHO?

WHAT?

WHEN?

MAIN IDEA:

WHERE?

HOW?

WHY?

119

©Jo Gusman, New Horizons In Education, Inc.

JO'S RECOMMENDED BOOKS AND ARTICLES
ASSESSMENT, BILINGUALISM, BRAIN RESEARCH, POLICY, SECOND LANGUAGE ACQUISITION

Armstrong, Thomas. Multiple Intelligences In The Classroom. Alexandria, Virginia: ASCD, 1994.

Asher, J.J. Learning Another Language Through Actions (6th ed.). Los Gatos, CA: Sky Oaks Productions, 2000.

Assessment Resource Library. Bibliography on Assessment: English Language Learners (Rev. ed.). Portland, OR: Northwest Regional Educational Laboratory. 2000.

Au, Kathryn H. Literacy Instruction in Multicultural Settings. Fort Worth, Texas: HBJ, 1993.

August, Diane, Shanahan, Timothy. Developing Literacy in Second Language Learners: Report of the National Literacy Panel On Language-Minority Children and Youth. Lawrence Erlbaum Associates, Publishers. 2006

Bailey, Dr. Alison L. The Language Demands of School: Putting Academic English to the Test. Yale University Press. 2007

Bernhardt, E.B., & Kamil, M.L. Interpreting Relationships Between L1 and L2 Reading: Consolidating the Linguistic Threshold and Linguistic Interdependence Hypotheses. Applied Linguistics, 16(1), 15-34, 1995.

Berman, P., Minicucci, C., McLaughlin, B., Nelson, B., & Woodworth, K. School Reform and Student Diversity: Case Studies of Exemplary Practices for LEP Students. Washington, DC: National Clearinghouse for Bilingual Education. Retrieved March 4, 2003, from www.ncela.gwu.edu/miscpubs/schoolreform/.

Calderon, Margarita, Minaya-Rowe, Liliana. Designing and Implementing Two-Way Bilingual Programs. Corwin Press, 2003.

Campbell, Duane. Choosing Democracy: A Practical Guide To Multicultural Education. Prentice-Hall Inc., 1996

Carasquillo, A.L., & Rodriquez, V. Language Minority Students in the Mainstream Classroom (2nd ed.). Philadelphia, PA: Multilingual Matters, 2002.

Chamot, Anna Uhl and O'Malley, Michael J. The CALLA Handbook: Implementing the Cognitive Academic Language Learning Approach. Reading, MA: Addison-Wesley, 1994.

Costantino. M. (with St. Charles, J., Tepper, S., & Baird, E). Reading and Second Language Learners: Research Report. Olympia, WA: Evergreen State college, Evergreen Center for Education Improvement. 1999. www.evergreen.edu/ecei/reports/2ndLangLrners.doc

Crawford, James. Bilingual Education: History, Politics. Theory. and Practice. Los Angeles, Bilingual Educational Services, 12989

Crawford, Leslie. Language and Literacv Learning in Multicultural Classrooms. Massachusetts: Allyn and Bacon, 1993.

Cummins, J. Schooling and Language Minority Students: A Theoretical Framework. Los Angeles, CA: Evaluation, Dissemination and Assessment Center California State University, Los Angeles, 1981.

Diaz-Rico, and Kathryn Z. Weed. The Cross-Cultural. Language. and Academic Development Handbook: A Complete K-12 Reference Guide. Massachusetts: Allyn and Bacon, 1995.

Doherty, R. W., Hilberg, R. S., Pinal, A., & Tharp, R.G. Five Standards and Student Achievement. NABE Journal of Research and Practice, 2003. 1(1), 1-24. www.uc.edu/njrp/pdfs/Doherty.pdf

Echevarria, J., Vogt, M., & Short, D. Making Content Comprehensible for English Language Learners. The SIOP Model. Boston, MA: Allyn & Bacon. 2000.

Echevarria, Jana and Graves, Anne. Sheltered Content Instruction. Allyn and Bacon, 1998.

Freeman, David and Yvonne. Between Worlds: Access to Second Language Acquisition. Portsmouth, NH: Heinemann, 1994.

Freeman, David and Yvonne. Essential Linguistics: What You Need To Know To Teach Reading, ESL, Spelling, Phonics, Grammar. Heinemann, 2004.

Whole Language for Second Language Learners. Portsmouth, NH: Heinemann, 1992.

Garcia, G.N. Lessons From Research: What Is The Length of Time It Takes Limited English Proficient Students To Acquire English and Succeed In An All-English Classroom? (NCBE Issue Brief No. 5). Washington, D.C.: National Clearinghouse for Bilingual Education. 2000. www.ncela.gwu.edu/ncbepubs/issuebriefs/ib5.htm

Garcia, Gilbert G. English Learners: Reaching The Highest Level of English Literacy. International Reading Association. 2003.

Gardner, Howard. Frames of Mind: New York, N.Y., A Basic Books, 1983.

Gibbons, Pauline. Learning to Learn in a Second Language. Portsmouth, NH: Heinemann, 1991.

Gibbons, Pauline. Scaffolding Language, Scaffolding Learning: Teaching Second Language Learners in the Mainstream Classroom. Portsmouth, NH: Heinemann, 2002.

Gusman, Jo. Practical Strategies for Accelerating the Literacy Skills and Content Learning of Your ESL Students. New Horizons In Education, Inc. Sacramento, CA, 2003.

Gusman, Jo. Differentiated Instruction for the English Language Learner: Best Practices To Use With Your Students (K-12). (Video and View Guide). National Professional Resources, Inc. Port Chester, NY, 2004.

Gusman, Jo. Multiple Intelligences and the Second Language Learner (video). National Professional Resources, Inc. Port Chester, NY, 1998.

Gusman, Jo. Multiple Intelligences and the Second Language Learner. A Resource Handbook. New Horizons In Education, Inc. Sacramento, CA, 2003.

Gusman, Jo. Optimizing Intelligences: Thinking. Emotion. and Creativity. (video) National Professional Resources, Inc. Port Chester, NY, 1998.

Gusman, Jo. Every Teacher - A Teacher of English Language Learners. The Video Journal-School Improvement Network. 2006. (Elementary and Secondary editions)

Hakuta, Kenji, Butler, Y.G. & Witt, D. How Long Does It Take English Learners to Attain Proficiency? Santa Barbara, CA: University of California, Linguistic Minority Research Institute, 2000.

Hakuta, Kenji, and Ellen Bialystok. In Other Words: The Science and Psychology of Second-Language Acquisition. New York, New York, 1994.

Hamayan, E.V. & Perlman, R. Helping Language Minority Students After They Exit from Bilingual/ESL Programs: A Handbook for Teachers (NCBE Program Information Guide Series No, 1). Washington, D.C.: National Clearinghouse for Bilingual Education, 1990. www.ncela.gwu.edu/ncbepubs/pigs/pig1.htm

Hart, Leslie, Olsen, Karen. Human Brain Human Learning. Books For Educators. Kent, Washington, 2002.

Hayes, Curtis, Robert Bahruth, Carolyn Kessler. Literacy Con Cariño. Portsmouth, NH: Heineman, 1991.

Herrell, A.A. Fifty Strategies for Teaching English Language Learners. Upper Saddle River, NJ: Pearson, Merrill Prentice Hall, 2003

Jameson, J. Three Principles for Success: English Language Learners In Mainstream Content Classes. (From Theory to Practice Issue No. 6). Tampa, FL: Center for Applied Linguistics, Region XIV Comprehensive Center, 1998. www.cal.org/cc14/ttp6.htm

Jarrett, D. The Inclusive Classroom: Teaching Mathematics and Science to English Language Learners. Portland, OR: Northwest Regional Educational Laboratory. 1999. www.nwrel.org/msec/just_good/8/index/html

Jensen, Eric. Teaching With The Brain In Mind. Alexandria, VA. ASCD, 1998.

Kagan, Spencer and Miquel. Multiple Intelligences: The Complete MI Book. Kagan Cooperative Learning. San Clemente, CA, 1998.

Kindler, A.L. Survey of the States Limited English Proficient Students and Available Educational Programs and Services: 2000-2001 Summary Report. Washington, D.C.: U.S. Department of Education, Office of English Language Acquisition, Language Enhancement and Academic Achievement for Limited English Proficient Students. 2002

Kovalik, Susan and Olsen Karen. Exceeding Expectations: A User's Guide To Implementing Brain Research In The Classroom. Kent, Washington, Books For Educators, 1999.

Krashen, S. Second Language Acquisition and Second Language Learning. New York, NY: Pergamon Press. London: Pergamon Press, 1981.

Krashen, S. Principles and Practice in Second Language Acquisition. New York: Pergamon Press, 1982.

Krashen, S. and T. Terrell. The Natural Approach: Language Acquisition in the Classroom. Hayward, CA: Alemany Press, 1983.

Law, Barbara, Mary Eckes. The More Than Just Surviving Handbook: ESL For Every Classroom Teacher. Winnipeg, Canada: Peguis Publishers, 1990.

Loop, C. What Tests Are Available That Measure The Yearly Academic Progress of English Language Learners? (AskNCELA No. 26). Washington, D.C.: National Clearinghouse for English Language Acquisition and Language Instruction Educational Programs, 2002. www.ncela.gwu.edu/askncela/26ayptests.htm

Martinez, R.D. Assessment: A Developmental Guide-Book for Teachers of English Language Learners. Portland, OR: Northwest Regional Educational Laboratory, 2002.

Nelson, G.L. Culture's Role In Reading Comprehension: A Schema Theoretical Approach. Journal of Reading, 30, 424-429, 1987.

Nevarez, Sandra, Raquel C. Mireles, Norma Ramirez. Experiences With Literature: A Thematic Whole Language Model for the K-3 Bilingual Classroom. Menlo Park, CA. Addison-Wesley, 1990.

Office for Civil Rights. Programs for English Language Learners: Resource Materials for Planning and Self-Assessments. Washington, D.C. Department of Education, 1999. www.ed.gov/offices/OCR/ELL/index.html

Peregoy, Suzanne and Owen Boyle. Reading. Writing. & Learning In ESL. White Plains, NY: Longman, 1993.

Perez, Bertha, and Maria Torres-Guzman. Learning In Two Worlds: An Integrated Spanish/English Biliteracy Approach. White Plains, NY: Longman, 1992.

Petitto, L.A. On The Biological Foundations of Human Language. In K. Emmorey & H. Lane (Eds.), The Signs of Language Revisited: An Anthology to Honor Ursula Bellugi and Edward Klima (pp. 447-471). Mahwah, NJ: Lawrence Erlbaum, 2000.

Reed, Bracken, & Railsback, Jennifer. Strategies and Resources for Mainstream Teachers of English Language Learners, Bracken Reed. Portland, OR: Northwest Regional Educational Laboratory, 2003.

Region X Equity Assistance Center. Improving Education For Immigrant Students: A Resource Guide for K-12 Educators in the Northwest and Alaska. Portland, OR: Northwest Regional Educational Laboratory, 1998. www.nwrel.org/cnorse/booklets/immigration/

Short, Deborah J. Newcomer Programs: An Educational Alternative for Secondary Immigrant Students. Education and Urban Society, 34(2), 173-198. 2002. Center for Applied Linguistics. Washington, D.C.: 2002. See CREDE Newcomers Project. www.cal.org/crede/newcomer.htm

Short Deborah J., Fitzsimmons, Shannon. Double the Work: Challenges and Solutions To Acquiring Language and Academic Literacy for Adolescent English Language Learners. Alliance for Excellent Education. Carnegie Corporation of New York, 2007.

Singleton, Glenn, Linton, Curtis. Courageous Conversations About Race: A Field Guide For Achieving Equity In Schools. Corwin Press, 2006.

Spangenberg-Urbschat, Karen and Robert Prichard. Kids Come In All Languages: Reading Instruction for ESL Students. Newark, Delaware: IRA, 1994.

Sylwester, Robert. A Celebration of Neurons: An Educator's Guide To The Human Brain. Alexandria, Virginia: ASCD, 1995.

Teele, Dr. Sue. The Multiple Intelligences School. (Book) Redlands, CA. Dr. Sue Teele and Associates, 1997.

The Multiple Intelligences School. (Video) National Professional Resources, Inc. Port Chester, NY, 1998.

Thonis, Eleanor. The English-Spanish Connection. Santillana, 1983, 2005.

Rainbows of Intelligences: Raising Student Performance Through Multiple Intelligences. Redlands, CA. Dr. Sue Teele and Associates, 1999.

Rainbows of Intelligences: Raising Student Performance Through Multiple Intelligences. (Video) National Professional Resources, Inc. Port Chester, NY, 1998.

Thomas, W.P., & Collier, V. School Effectiveness for Language Minority Students. (NCBE Resource Collection Series No. 9). Washington, D.C. National Clearinghouse for Bilingual Education, 1997. www.ncela.gwu.edu/ncbepubs/resource/effectiveness/

Thonis, Eleanor. The English-Spanish Connection. Northvale, New Jersey: Santillana, 1983.

U.S. Department of Education. Language Instruction for Limited English Proficient and Immigrant Students. (Title III of the No Child Left Behind Act of 2001, PL 107-110). Washington, D.C.: Author, 2001.

Whitmore, Kathryn, and Caryl Crowell. Inventing A Classroom: Life In A Bilingual Whole Language Learning Community. York, Maine: Stenhouse Publishing, 1994.

Wrigley, P. The Help! Kit: A Resource Guide for Secondary Teachers of Migrant English Language Learners. Oneonta, NY: ESCORT. 2001
www.escort.org/products/HSclc1

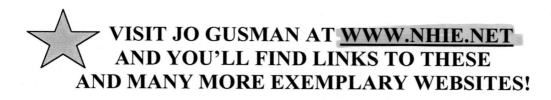

VISIT JO GUSMAN AT WWW.NHIE.NET
AND YOU'LL FIND LINKS TO THESE
AND MANY MORE EXEMPLARY WEBSITES!

JO GUSMAN'S RECOMMENDED BILINGUAL/MULTICULTURAL/ESL WEBSITES

► ADVOCACY/LANGUAGE POLICY/ELL RESEARCH

Center for Adult English Language Acquisition *(formerly the National Center for ESL Literacy Education)*   http://www.cal.org/caela/

Center for Applied Linguistics   www.cal.org

Center for Equity and Excellence in Education Test Database
http://r3cc.ceee.gwu.edu/standards_assessments/database.htm

Center for Language Minority Education and Research   www.clmer.csulb.edu/

Center for Multilingual Multicultural Research (CMMR)
http://www.usc.edu/dept/education/CMMR/

Center for Research on Education, Diversity, Excellence   www.crede.ucsc.edu

CREDE'S Five Standards of Effective Pedagogy
www.crede.ucsc.edu/standards/standards.html

Clearinghouse on Languages and Linguistics
http://www.cal.org/resources/update.html

Directory of Two-Way Immersion Programs   www.cal.org/twi/directory

Jim Cummins' Second Language Learning and Literacy Development Web
www.iteachilearn.com/cummins/

Language Policy and Language Rights   www-rcf.usc.edu/~cmmr/Policy.html

Language Policy Web Site and Emporium
http://ourworld.compuserve.com/homepages/JWCRAWFORD/

Linguistic Minority Research Association   http://lmri.ucsb.edu/

*Jo Gusman's website – www.nhie.net

Linguistic Minority Research Association – Minority Resources
http://www.hamptonu.edu/bsrc/CMSE/olinks.html

National Association of Bilingual Education   www.nabe.org

National Center for Research on Evaluation, Standards, and Student Testing
www.cresst.org

National Center for Research on Cultural Diversity and Second Language Learning
http://www.cal.org/Archive/projects/ncrcdsll.htm

National Clearinghouse for English Language Acquisition and Language Instruction Educational Programs *(formerly the National Clearinghouse for Bilingual Education)*
www.ncela.gwu.edu

NCELA Individual State Data   http://www.ncela.gwu.edu/policy/allstates/

✳ **Northwest Regional Educational Laboratory Equity Center**   www.nwrel.org

Office for Civil Rights   www.ed.gov/about/offices/list/ocr/ell/index.html

Portraits of Success (database of successful bilingual education programs)
www.alliance.brown.edu/pubs/pos/

U.S. Department of Education's Office of English Language Acquisition, Language Enhancement, and Academic Achievement for Limited English Proficient Students (OELA)
http://www.ed.gov/about/offices/list/oela/index.html?src=oc

Research on Language Minority Education
http://www.ncela.gwu.edu/pubs/reports/bestevidence/research.htm

Sheltered Instruction Observation Protocol   www.siopinstitute.net

Teachers of English to Speakers of Other Languages   www.tesol.org

West Ed *(Authors of "The Map of Standards for English Learners: Integrating Instruction and Assessment of English Language Development and English Language Arts Standards")*
www.wested.org

What Works Clearinghouse   www.w-w-c.org

*Jo Gusman's website – www.nhie.net

► PRACTICAL IDEAS/LESSON PLANS/ RESOURCE MATERIALS

✴ **1-Language**   www.1-language.com

1-Language.com Flashcards and ESL Activities
                              http://www.1-language.com/eslflashcards/index.htm

4 Teachers ESL Links Page   www.4teachers.org

Activities for ESL Students   http://a4esl.org

✴ **BBC English**   www.bbc.co.uk/worldservice/learningenglish

Bilingual Teacher Store   www.bilingualteacherstore.com

Boggles World   www.bogglesworld.com

Breaking News English- ESL/EFL Lesson Plans For Current Affairs
                              www.breakingnewsenglish.com

CNN Newsroom and Worldview for ESL/CNN Student News
                              http://lc.byuh.edu/CNN-N/CNN-N.html

Dave's ESL Café   www.eslcafe.com

Dave's ESL Café's Web Guide   www.eslcafe.com/search/index.html

Disney Song Lyrics   www.geocities.com/Broadway/Stage/7840/select.htm

EduHound Español   www.eduhound.com/espanol

✴ **English As A Second Language**   www.rong-chang.com

English Club   www.englishclub.com

English Learner.Com   www.englishlearner.com

English Learner Mentor   http://elm.borderlink.org/

✴ **English To Go**   www.english-to-go.com

ESL All International   www.eslall.com

ESL/Bilingual/Foreign Language Lesson Plans and Resources
                              http://www.csun.edu/~hcedu013/eslindex.html

ESL Games/Edutainment   www.eslgames.com

*Jo Gusman's website – www.nhie.net

ESL Grammar Links for ESL Students
http://www.research.umbc.edu/~rschwart/links.htm

ESL Lessons and Flashcards　　　　　　　　　　www.esl-images.com

ESL Lounge　　　　　　　　　　　　　　　　　www.esl-lounge.com

ESL Resources　　　　　　　http://members.aol.com/Jakajk/ESLLessons.html

ESL Through Music　　　　　　www.forefrontpublishers.com/eslmusic

English Outlook: Online Magazine　　　　　www.englishoutlook.com

ESL Wonderland　　　　　　　　　　　　www.eslwonderland.com

Everything ESL　　　　　　　　　　www.everythingesl.net/lessons/

Holiday Zone: Activities for English Language Learners
www.theholidayzone.com

Interesting Things for ESL Students　　　　www.manythings.org

Interesting Things for ESL Students to Read
www.iei.uiuc.edu/web.pages/readinglist.html

Internet Picture Dictionary (multilingual picture dictionary) www.pdictionary.com

Internet Resources for Language Teachers and Learners
www.fredriley.org.uk/call/langsite/

It's Elemental (The Periodic Table of Elements)
http://education.jlab.org/itselemental/

Jo Gusman, New Horizons In Education Inc.
　　Speakers Bureau and Educational Materials　　　　www.nhie.net

Karin's ESL Party Land　　　　　　　www.eslpartyland.com

Middle Web　　　　　　　　　　　www.middleweb.com

New York Times Learning Network　　　www.nytimes.com/learning/

Teaching Diverse Learners　　　http://www.alliance.brown.edu/tdl/index.shtml

TESL/TEFL/TESOL/ESL/EFL/ESOL Links　　　http://iteslj.org/links/

Pam's ESL Classroom　　　　　　www.pamseslclassroom.com

Parlez Vous ? (French)　　　　　　　www.parlez-vous.org

*Jo Gusman's website – www.nhie.net

Planning Instruction for English Language Development: A Knowledge Base of Teaching Strategies

http://coe.sdsu.edu/people/jmora/MoraModules/ELDInstruction.htm

Songs For Teaching: Using Music To Promote Learning

www.songsforteaching.com

Teach With Movies   www.teachwithmovies.com

The Educators Reference Desk   www.eduref.org

We Speak English   www.wespeakenglish.com/

► READING/LANGUAGE ARTS/BILITERACY

Bilingual Reading Instruction   www.ncela.gwu.edu/pathways/reading/

Connie Prevatte's Theory Into Practice: Literacy In The Middle Grades

www.connieprevatte.com

International Reading Association   www.reading.org

Literacy Matters   www.literacymatters.org

National Literacy Panel on Language Minority Children and Youth (NLP)

www.cal.org/natl-lit-panel/

Read Write Think   www.readwritethink.org

The Knowledge Loom: Adolescent Literacy In The content Areas

www.knowledgeloom.org

The Textmapping Project: A Resource for Teachers Improving Reading Comprehension Skills Instruction   www.textmapping.org

► MORE ESL AND EFL GAMES

GOOGLE IT! Type in "ESL or EFL games and lesson plans"or "English Language Development lesson plans and strategies." This will lead you to a long list of websites filled with lots of practical ideas.

*Jo Gusman's website – www.nhie.net

► **SPANISH/MULTILINGUAL RESOURCES – BOOK VENDOR**

Mariuccia Iaconi Book Imports   (415) 821-1216
970 Tennessee Street
San Francisco, CA 94107   www.mibibook.com/contactus.html

► **SPANISH/MULTILINGUAL RESOURCES – WEB SITES**

Algunos Lugares en Español   www.kn.pacbell.com/wired/Algunos/

Biblioteca Infantil   www.storyplace.org/sp/eel/eel.asp

Bibliography of Chicano Literature   http://instech.tusd.k12.az.us/Raza/links.asp

Bilingual Books for Kids   www.bilingualbooks.com

Center for the Study of Books in Spanish   www.csusm.edu/csb/english

CNN en Español   http://www.cnn.com/espanol/

ESCUELA.NET   www.escuela.net

EspanOle! Pagina Principal   www.espanole.org/

Internet Resources for Language Teachers and Learners
      www.fredriley.org.uk/call/langsite/

Juegos y Canciones Para Los Niños   www.hevanet.com/dshivers/juegos

K-3 Resources for Bilingual Educators   www.estrellita.com/k3.bil.res.html

Learn Spanish   www.studyspanish.com/

Sitio Infantil   www.globalpc.net/entretenimiento/juegos

Spanish Lessons on the Web, Links   www.whitebuffalos.net/Spanish/links.htm

Spanish Teacher Resources   www.geocites.com/sra_rk/worldlang_resources0.htm

Trabalenguas (Spanish Tongue Twisters)   www.uebersetzung.at/twister/es.htm

UCLA Language Materials Project: Teaching Resources for Less Commonly
Taught Languages   www.lmp.ucla.edu/

Web Spanish Lessons   www.june29.com/Spanish/

*Jo Gusman's website – www.nhie.net

► SPANISH /MULTICULTURAL/MULTILINGUAL SEARCH ENGINES

Alta Vista Spain	www.altavista.com
Arabic search engine	www.4arabs.com
Auyantepui (Venzuela)	www.auyantepui.com
EduHound Español	http://www.eduhound.com/espanol
Euroseek (European)	www.euroseek.com
Galeon	www.galeon.com/aprenderaaprender/general/indice
GauchoNet (Argentina)	www.gauchonet.com
Google	www.google.com
Hikyaku (Japanese)	www.hikyaku.com/trans/jengineg.html
Hispavista	www.hispavista.com
Lycos	www.lycos.com
Marjorie Chan's China Links (China)	http://chinalinks.osu.edu/
Mexicoweb (Mexico)	www.mexicoweb.com
Mexmaster (Mexico)	www.mexmaster.com
National U.S. – Arab Chamber of Commerce	www.nusacc.org
Quepasa	www.quepasa.com
Russian search engines	www.searchenginecolossus.com/Russia.html
Spanish About	www.spanish.about.com
Terra (Spain)	http://www.terra.es/
Uruguay Total (Uruguay)	www.uruguaytotal.com
Yagua (Paraguay)	www.yagua.com
Yahoo! (available in country specific versions)	www.yahoo.com
YUPI (Latin American search engine)	http://www.yupimsn.com/

*Jo Gusman's website – www.nhie.net

► TRANSLATION SITES AND SOFTWARE

All Words   www.allwords.com

Alta Vista Babel Fish Translation Service   http://babelfish.altavista.com

Systran Information and Translation Technologies   www.systransoft.com

The Human Languages Page   www.ilovelanguages.com

Your Dictionary   www.yourdictionary.com

► REFUGEE IMMIGRANT/CULTURES/DEMOGRAPHIC INFORMATION

CIA – The World Factbook
           http://www.odci.gov/cia/publications/factbook/index.html

Culture Grams   www.culturegrams.com

The United Nations Refugee Agency (UNHCR)   www.unhcr.ch

United States Citizenship and Immigration Services (Immigrant and Refugee Statistics)   www.uscis.gov

U.S. Department of Health and Human Services – Office of Refugee Resettlement
          www.acf.dhhs.gov/programs/orr/

Visit a Refugee Camp (curriculum on refugee issues)   www.refugeecamp.org

► RESEARCH SITES FOR ESL STUDENTS

Content Area Instruction and Current Events   www.proteacher.com

Human Resource Institute   www.hrinstitute.info/LinksDem.asp

Questia – World's Largest ESL Online Library   www.Questia.com

► STATE AND SUBJECT AREA EDUCATIONAL STANDARDS

Developing Educational Standards   http://edstandards.org/Standards.html

*Jo Gusman's website – www.nhie.net

MY QUESTION

DRAW OR WRITE THE ANSWER

IMPLEMENTATION IDEAS

1.

2.

3.

RESEARCH-BASED EDUCATIONAL RESOURCES

NEW HORIZONS IN EDUCATION, INC.

SUPPORT, GUIDANCE, AND LEADERSHIP THROUGHOUT

THE PROFESSIONAL DEVELOPMENT PROCESS

2007 CATALOG
Using Research-Based Materials
This Catalog Provides For:

★ *English Language Learners*
   Pre K — Adult

★ *Literacy/Bi-literacy*

★ *Differentiated Instruction*

★ *Brain-Based Learning*

★ *Multiple Intelligences*

★ *Cooperative Learning*

★ *Diversity*

★ **NoChild**
   LeftBehind

"Always in Touch with the Future"
Jo Gusman, President

Visit us on-line at: www.nhie.net

Scott Anthony, CEO of NHIE and Jo Gusman, Educational Consultant and President of NHIE

JO GUSMAN grew up in a Spanish speaking farm-working family who experienced the challenges that non-English speakers face in the United States. Based on her childhood experiences as a "limited English speaker", she truly understands the complexities and multiple variables that surround the English language learner. Jo began her teaching career in 1974 as a bilingual instructional assistant, and later attended California State University, Sacramento where she received her Bilingual Cross-Cultural teaching credential and Masters. Jo was a Bilingual Education teacher for many years, and in 1981 her career led her to the nationally known Newcomer School, where Jo worked in a multilingual setting with refugee and immigrant K-8 students. It is there where she developed her many brain-based ESL strategies. Because of her extensive experience and exceptional work with English language learners, she has been featured on national television, and is the recipient of numerous awards, including President Ronald Reagan's recognition for teaching excellence. Presently, Jo provides educators, students, parents, and policy makers with professional development language and literacy seminars throughout the world.

Jo's husband, **SCOTT ANTHONY**, grew up in Lexington, Nebraska, in a farm family who valued education. His mom was a one-room schoolhouse teacher and his dad, a farmer, served as President of the school board of their rural school district. Scott, a graduate of the University of Nebraska, College of Engineering, went on to specialize in construction management, with a specialty in church building. Scott provided construction management services to over 200 church projects throughout the United States and abroad for 18 years.

After many years of working independently, Scott and Jo came together to create their educational consulting firm, **New Horizons In Education, Inc.** It is their vision and intention to provide their clients with practical, research-based ideas, inspiration, and a vision that all children and adults are highly creative and intelligent, and can be successful in all aspects of their lives, regardless of race, gender, or socio-economic level.

We look forward to partnering with you to provide a quality education for all children and adults.

"Support, guidance, and leadership throughout the professional development process."

"Always in Touch with the Future"
Jo Gusman, President

www.nhie.net

Jo Gusman's Workshop Resource Handbooks

The following handbooks accompany Jo Gusman's workshops. While they are available for sale, these items are "workshop resource handbooks" which accompany Jo's seminars.

NEW SEMINAR!!

Accelerating Your ELL Students' Reading Comprehension, Vocabulary Development and Reading Fluency

Jo Gusman

Based on No Child Left Behind-*Reading First* legislation and the recommendations from the *National Reading Panel*, Jo's newest seminar and handbook are designed to help teachers in grades 3-8 strengthen the reading comprehension, vocabulary development, and reading fluency of their ELL students. The handbook is filled with dozens of practical research-based strategies and processes, blackline masters, and an extensive bibliography of current research-based materials and Internet sites.

Price: $24.95
Order: #B-RC

Practical Strategies for Accelerating the Literacy Skills and Content Learning of Your ELL Students

Jo Gusman

This handbook from Jo Gusman's most requested workshop is constantly updated by Jo herself as she integrates research consistent with findings from the No Child Left Behind Act and practical ideas from her many years of teaching students from a multitude of linguistic backgrounds. Filled with graphic organizers, theories explained, ready-to-use ideas, and numerous resources, this handbook serves as an invaluable reference guide.

Price: $24.95
Order: #B-ESL

Practical Strategies for Accelerating the Literacy Skills and Content Learning of Your ESL Students—Workshop Audiocassette & Handbook Package

Jo Gusman

Learn new and innovative techniques for helping your ELL students acquire key literacy skills with this six audiocassette package accompanied by Jo's comprehensive handbook. You will receive a wide array of ELL literacy building strategies, descriptions of specific and proven teaching strategies for making content material more comprehensible, numerous ideas for creating successful second language acquisition environments, and an extensive bibliography. Join thousands of appreciative teachers across North America already currently using Jo's strategies which are known for their practical value in building success for second language learners!

Six Audiocassettes & Handbook
Price: $89.00
Order: #A-ESG-0703
4 hours, 6 minutes

The Top 5 Things You Can Do For Your English Language Learners and Their Teachers Seminar for Site and Central Office Administrators

Jo Gusman

Call us to schedule this workshop!

As an accompaniment to Jo's administrator workshop of the same title, this resource handbook guides participants through her presentation answering the following questions and needs:
1. Begin with the Laws!
2. What Is The Affective Filter and How Can I Create a Brain-Compatible Learning Environment for the ELL and Their Families?
3. How Do You Make Your Input Comprehensible?
4. We Need A Comprehensive Program For These Students — Implement Jo's FOUNDATION-FRAMEWORK-TOOLS Program Model
5. One Size Does Not Fit All — Understanding Differentiated Instruction and 8 Different Ways to Meet ELL Needs In the Classroom — Implement the Multiple Intelligences Theory Into Your Curriculum and Instruction Model

Price: $24.95
Order: #B-TF

To order call Toll Free 1-800-573-NHIE

Jo Gusman's Workshops

New Horizons In Education, Inc. is proud to offer the following seminars by our featured consultant, Jo Gusman. Each seminar is unique and offers a wealth of practical ideas for teachers, administrators, teacher trainers, instructional assistants and parents. Please contact us to schedule your 1-3 day seminar, keynote address, or long-term professional development partnership.

§ Practical Strategies for Accelerating the Literacy Skills and Content Learning Of Your ELL Students

§ Accelerating Your ELL Students' Reading Comprehension, Vocabulary Development and Reading Fluency (Grades 3-8)

§ Foundation-Frameworks-Tools: A Step-by-Step Plan for Developing a Brain-Based Program for ELL

§ Diverse Brains, Diverse Learners: Understanding The Complex World Of Your English Language Learners—Keynote

§ Multiple Intelligences and the English Language Learner

§ Bi-Literacy: Multiple Paths To Success: Research-Based Bi-Literacy Instruction For ALL Students

§ Meeting Your State Standards With Confidence

§ Creating Inclusive Schools For English Language Learners And Their Families—Keynote & Workshop for School Secretaries, Bus Drivers and other Support Personnel

§ Helping Your Child Succeed In School (Presented in Spanish; Parent Workshop)

Visit our website to learn more about each individual workshop, and please contact us to find out how we can tailor each workshop to fit the needs of your school or district!

"Always in Touch with the Future"
Jo Gusman, President

www.nhie.net • info@nhie.net • **T:** 916-482-4405 • **F:** 916-482-4433

Toll Free: (800) 573-NHIE *or* (800) 573-6443

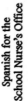

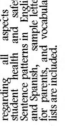
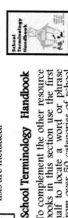

Buenos Dias:
Beginning Spanish for Teachers of Spanish Speaking Students
Book/Cassette Package
Dr. Pamela J. Sharpe

Title II

This program will help teachers who need to communicate in the Spanish vernacular with students whose English is not fluent. 24 lessons deal with greeting a child, giving directions in the classroom, and more. Includes four 60-minute audio-cassettes with script and more than 370 flash cards to help the learner's memory retention. *Paperback with four audio-cassettes; 288 pages*

Price: $42.95
Order: #A-8118-8

"It is a privilege to share my book *Buenos Dias: Spanish for Hispanic Students* with Jo Gusman's workshop participants. I know that being able to communicate in Spanish with your students will open their minds and hearts to everything else in your classroom, and will give you a deep insight into the world of a language learner. Best wishes to you all." – *Dr. Pamela Sharpe, author of Buenos Dias*

Learn Spanish the Fast and Fun Way
Book/CD Package
Gene Hammitt;
Heywood Wald, Coordinating Editor

Title II

Here's how to learn Spanish painlessly for vacationing, shopping, making phone calls, dining, sightseeing, and generally getting around Spanish cities and countrysides. Vocabulary cards, gummed labels and other fun-learning features come as part of the book.

Price: $49.95
Order: #A7527-0

"Great for Spanish speaking parents wanting to learn English!" -Jo Gusman

Aprenda Ingles Facil Y Rapido
Book/Cassette Package, Second Edition
Dente Arnaldo

Title III

As part of the Fast and Fun Way book/audio-cassette sets, this package gives Spanish speakers the added advantage of learning English by letting them hear and pronounce the language as it is spoken. (Grades 6-9) Vinyl Case / 288 Pages

Price: $39.95
Order: #A-7289-1

GREAT FOR PARENTS AND YOUR PIRC AREA! *(Parent Information & Resource Center)*

SPANISH *in 10 minutes a day*
CHINESE *in 10 minutes a day*
ARABIC *in 10 minutes a day*
INGLÉS *en 10 minutos al día*
RUSSIAN *in 10 minutes a day*
English for Spanish

10 Minutes A Day
Spanish, Russian, Chinese or Arabic Available

Title III

A complete language-learning kit! Learn a language in 25 easy steps. The purpose of this book is to give you an immediate speaking ability in a foreign language, together with some practical and cultural tips. Each book includes expanded contents, all-new illustrations, sticky labels and flash cards, menu guide, puzzles & games, color illustrations, and a glossary. Each step has its own element of fun. Practical, fast & easy—and most important, it works!

	Price	Order
Inglés	$19.95	#B-ING10
Arabic	$19.95	#B-ARA10
Russian	$19.95	#B-RUS10
Spanish	$18.95	#B-SPA10
Chinese	$19.95	#B-CHI10

Price: $24.95
Order: #A-7272-7

BEST SELLER!

Spanish for Educators
Book/Cassette Package
William C. Harvey, M.S.

Title II

This is a highly informal, entirely practical and down-to-earth approach to Spanish. Produced to help educators speak and comprehend Spanish in the classroom and for counseling purposes. Among matters covered are: Classroom instruction, discipline, health care, educational administration, special needs, and extracurricular activities. *(2) 90-minute audio-cassettes + book*

HELP! They Don't Speak English
A Basic Translator For Classroom Survival
Tonnie Martinez, Ph.D.

Title III

This educational tool is a must for every teacher who needs to know some basic school classroom phrases in Spanish. The colorful flip book offers teachers the phrases in English, Spanish, and phonetic translations that anyone can use during classroom situations, P.E., recess and emergencies.

Price: $19.95
Order: #B-HTD

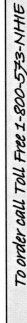
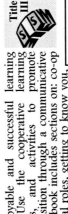
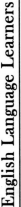

ELL Materials for Administrators

NEW!

Title III

Designing and Implementing Two-Way Bilingual Programs:
A Step-by-Step Guide for Administrators, Teachers, and Parents
Margarita Espino Calderon & Liliana Minaya-Rowe

Two-way bilingual education helps children maintain their cultural language as well as learn a new language—an invaluable skill in an increasingly integrated world. Designing and Implementing Two-Way Bilingual Programs provides essential elements to help your students gain literacy in two languages, increase cross-cultural understanding, and meet high levels of achievement in all core academic areas. This indispensable handbook also includes strategies for building learning communities for dual-language teachers, professional development plans that meet the specific needs of dual-language programs, and tips for involving parents.

Price: $34.95
Order: #B-4566-0

NEW!

Standards-Based Instruction and Assessment for English Language Learners
Mary Ann Lachat

Standards-Based Instruction and Assessment for English Language Learners explores the issues that must be addressed to ensure the academic success of English Language Learners (ELLs). Providing an overview of what standards-based educational reforms means for the fast-growing population of ELLs in America's schools, author Mary Ann Lachat offers practical guidelines to help school administrators and classroom teachers implement effective practices for culturally diverse learners. The manual includes useful tools for conducting a school-wide assessment and designing professional development plans for teachers. Bridging research to policy and practice implications, this Title III unique manual examines:

- The characteristics of ELLs in America's schools
- How language and culture affect learning
- Language development issues for ELLs
- What teachers need to know about assessment for ELLs
- Standards-based learning practices that support the success of ELLs

Price: $24.95
Order: #B-3893-1

Find more titles on our website!
www.nhie.net

Price: $29.95
Order: #B-194

Price: $32.95
Order: #B-3949-0

Also see our staff development videos on pages 20-21!

Price: $35.95
Order: #B-455

❖ Need more for ELL? Try these materials!
English Language Learners

Title III

All items on this page qualify for Title III funds!

Making Content Comprehensible for English Language Learners The SIOP Model
Jana Echevarria, MaryEllen Vogt, & Deborah J. Short

Reading, Writing and Learning in ESL
Suzanne Peregoy and Owen Boyle

Praised for its strong research base, engaging style, and inclusion of specific teaching ideas, this Fourth Edition provides a wealth of practical strategies for promoting literacy and language development in K-12 English language learners. This book takes a unique approach by exploring contemporary language acquisition theory as it relates to instruction and providing suggestions and methods for motivating and involving English language learners.

Price: $63.95
Order: #B-4103

50 Strategies for Teaching English Language Learners
Adrienne Herrell & Michael Jordan

Explore 50 research-based, classroom-tested strategies that teachers can use to help ELL understand content materials while acquiring English language skills. All strategies are related to the national TESOL standards, and step-by-step instructions and concrete examples help you quickly and easily use the strategies in any K-12 classroom and subject.

Price: $34.95
Order: #B-50STR

Making Content Comprehensible presents a coherent, specific, field-tested model of sheltered instruction that specifies the features of a high-quality sheltered lesson that teaches content material to English learners. Each of the 30 items from the SIOP model are illustrated through vignettes. Three different lessons for each item are rated and discussed, allowing the book to be applied to a variety of content areas and grade levels.

Price: $39.95
Order: #B-3864

Vocabulary Improvement Program for English Language Learners and Their Classmates
Teresa Lively, M.S., Diane August, Ph.D., Catherine Snow, Ph.D., & Carla Mario, Ph.D.

Research studies have shown that students' vocabulary knowledge strongly correlates with their success in reading comprehension. Now teachers can give **fourth, fifth, and sixth graders** the crucial vocabulary practice they need with this three-volume curriculum — proven equally effective for English-language learners (ELLs) and students whose first language is English. This program uses innovative approaches to help students build a "toolbox" of skills that let them decipher the meanings of unfamiliar words with confidence.

Price: $49.95 each
Order: #B-6318 (4th)
#B-6326 (5th)
#B-6334 (6th)

NEW!

How to Explain a Brain:
An Educator's Handbook for Brain Terms and Cognitive Processes
Robert Slywester

Title II

This unique look into the marvelous brain uses language and descriptions that are accessible to readers, even those with just a limited understanding of biology. Discover how our brain is organized and develops, and how educators can use this emerging understanding of cognition to enhance student learning and the school environment. This ready-reference guide to essential concepts and terms in cognitive neurosciences includes:

- *Nearly 300 encyclopedic entries and cross references created to help educators understand key concepts about our brain's organization, development, and learning capabilities*
- *Eleven newly created anatomic models and illustrations that focus on key brain systems and functions*
- *References and recommended print and Internet resources*

Price: $32.95
Order: #B-7861-5

NEW!

12 Brain/Mind Learning Principles in Action:
The Fieldbook for Making Connections, Teaching and the Human Brain
Renate Nummela Caine, Geoffrey Caine, Carol McClintic, Karl Klimek

This new book from the Caines and their colleagues will introduce readers to their renowned 12 organizing principles for how the brain learns and how to use that knowledge for student learning. 12 Brain/Mind Learning Principles in Action is grouped around key teaching and learning fundamentals:

- *Climate for learning*
- *Instruction*
- *Student processing*

Title II

Linked to National Teaching Standards, this fieldbook builds the bridge from new brain research to classroom practice. With distinct elements for teachers and school leaders, it will facilitate adoption by whole learning communities.

Price: $34.95
Order: #B-0984-8

NEW!

Leading With the Brain in Mind:
101 Brain-Compatible Practices for Leaders
Michael H. Dickmann, Nancy Stanaford-Blair, & Anthea Rosati-Bojar

Effective leadership hinges not only on understanding the nature of human intelligence, but also, more importantly, on applying the principles that nurture it. Taking leaders from *knowledge* about the value of brain-based leadership, to *action* based on the best available research is what this inspiring guide is all about. Unique features of this text include:

- *Integrated intuitive reflection exercises*
- *Definition of leadership within the context of the 21st century*
- *Practical tips for understanding—and nurturing—the nature of intelligence*
- *A repertoire of 15 leadership strategies and 101 aligned practices*
- *Reasons and ways to cultivate a culture of learning and achievement*

Title II

Price: $32.95
Order: #B-3949-0

Building the Reading Brain, Pre-K–3
Patricia Wolfe & Pamela Nevills

NEW!

Research indicates that a student's future academic success can be predicted by his or her reading level at the end of third grade. Learning to read is a complex, gradual process that begins in infancy. Read about the development of the young brain, the acquisition of language as preparation for reading, and the nurturing and instruction process from birth to age eight.

Price: $28.95
Order: #B-3904-0

- *Activities to support phonemic awareness, phonics, vocabulary, comprehension, and fluency*
- *Applications of games, music, play, and instruction*
- *Intervention suggestions for children who are challenged or discouraged early readers*

How the Brain Learns to Read
David A. Sousa

NEW!

Learn what scientists have uncovered about how children develop spoken language and use spoken language abilities when learning to read. Complete with relevant brain diagrams and informative tables, this exciting new book examines critical concepts including:

Price: $39.95
Order: #B-0601-6

- *Understanding language acquisition and its relationship to reading*
- *Incorporating modern research findings in your classroom*
- *Recognizing and overcoming reading problems, including early intervention programs*
- *Content area reading with strategies to improve vocabulary and comprehension*
- *Developing a successful reading program that encourages teachers to be researchers*

Overcoming Barricades to Reading: A Multiple Intelligences Approach
Sue Teele

NEW!

Learn how to unlock the door to literacy by teaching to the individual and unique strengths of their students.

Price: $35.95
Order: #B-3140-6

- *New directions for teaching reading*
- *An overview of the brain's structure and how individual differences influence the reading process*
- *An examination of the theory of multiple intelligences and how its application can significantly increase the effectiveness of traditional reading and writing instructional methods*
- *Case studies, practical diagrams, maps and charts illustrating techniques that will improve decoding, comprehension, and writing skills*
- *Innovative strategies for teaching reading to English Language Learners*

Reading for Academic Success:
Powerful Strategies for Struggling, Average, and Advanced Readers (Gr. 7-12)
Richard W. Strong, Harvey F. Silver, Matthew J. Perini, Gregory M. Tuculescu

NEW!

Expressly designed for the secondary teacher, the down-to-earth approach and proven methods outlined can have a significant and far-reaching positive impact in any school—turning even average or below-average students into high-achieving, thoughtful readers.

Price: $29.95
Order: #B-7834-8

- *Exploration of the seven core reading challenges and corresponding strategies for success*
- *Tips for tailoring each strategy to distinct disciplines, from Science and Mathematics to English and Social Studies*
- *"Strategies for Struggling Readers" section in each chapter that highlights ways to meet the needs of students with learning disabilities and other special needs*
- *Practical applications that implement and reinforce research findings, including the five common characteristics of successful readers*

Brain-Based Education

Multiple Intelligences
The Complete MI Book
Dr. Spencer Kagan & Miguel Kagan
(All Grades)

Title I

This book is the single most comprehensive MI book available, helping you to promote academic success for all your students by using fun and easy MI strategies that match how all students learn best. You will learn to: stretch your students' multiple intelligences; help students build on their strengths to become smarter in many ways; help create a supportive learning environment in which students are appreciated for their multiple intelligences and celebrate the uniqueness of their classmates. These easy-to-master MI strategies make any lesson accessible to all intelligences, while developing and celebrating the unique pattern of intelligences in each student!

Price: $39.00
Order: #B-MITC

Multiple Intelligences
The Complete MI Book

OVER 160 MI STRATEGIES!

NEW!

Worksheets Don't Grow Dendrites: 20 Instructional Strategies That Engage the Brain
Marcia L. Tate

Worksheets Don't Grow Dendrites targets teachers as "growers of brain cells" and encourages them to make practical application of the findings of learning style theorists and neuroscientists. Tactile learners, spatial thinkers, and logical minds alike will become eager students as the strategies in this handbook are implemented. Marcia Tate demonstrates 20 strategies including:

Price: $27.95
Order: #B-3881-8

Title I, II

- Using humor and telling stories
- Implementing problem-based instruction
- Incorporating games into lessons
- Utilizing mnemonic devices and metaphors
- And even singing and dancing while learning

Brain Food: 100+ Games that Make Kids Think, Grades 4-12
Paul Fleisher, M.Ed.

NEW!

Be the one to make a difference in your students' thinking! With more than 100 games to choose from, Brain Food is your one-stop source for exploring the fun in learning. This compilation is filled with new as well as most traditional games, and most need little more than paper and pencil to get you started. Each game is classroom tested and tailored to enhance the intelligences of your students.

Title I, II

Price: $29.95
Order: #B-0721

Visit www.nhie.net for more titles addressing Brain-Based Education!

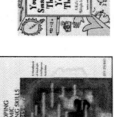

Overcoming Barricades to READING
Sue Teele
Price: $35.95
Order: #B-3140-6

You're Smarter Than You Think
Price: $15.95
Order: #B-773

DEVELOPING ... THINKING SKILLS
Price: $26.95
Order: #B-557

Teaching Comprehension and Exploring Multiple Literacies
Strategies from the *Reading Teacher*
Timothy V. Rasinsky, et al.

Whatever grade level, content, or texts you teach, your ultimate goal is to develop your students' understanding of what they read. The 29 articles in this anthology offer you a wealth of ideas to help your students comprehend different types of texts and literacies, from technology literacy to visual, theater, and music literacy. You'll find instructional strategies and activities on a wide range of topics, including narrative and expository texts, the K-W-L strategy, anticipation guides, graphic organizers, wordless picture books, shared books, the Internet as a teaching resource, and integrating music, reading and writing at the primary level.

Price: $16.95
Order: #-281

Classroom Strategies for Interactive Learning, Second Edition
Doug Buehl

This book provides middle school and high school educators with 45 literacy skill-building strategies that can easily be adapted for students at a variety of ability levels, emphasizing effective learning in content contexts. With the development of state and national achievement standards in reading, writing, social studies, mathematics, science, and other curricular areas, it is more important than ever for educators to develop the literacy skills of older students. The activities in this book will help you instill in your learners the skills and desire to read increasingly complex materials, and provide explicit instruction in reading comprehension and study strategies across the curriculum.

Price: $22.95
Order: #B-284

Comprehension Strategies for Middle Grade Learners
Charlotte Rose Sadler
Price: $16.95
Order: #B-292

Price: $29.95
Order: #B-194

Price: $29.95
Order: #B-50LIT

50 Literacy Strategies Step by Step

Single user license:
Price: $39.95
Order: #S-HFTS
Unlimited school license:
Price: $399.95
Order: #S-HFTU

Find more titles on our website!
www.nhie.net

Brain-Based Education–Videos

Title I

How Are Kids Smart?
Multiple Intelligences in the Classroom
Dr. Howard Gardner

Learn about M.I. theory, the seven intelligences, and observe first hand how teachers under the guidance of Dr. Howard Gardner have incorporated M.I. theory into their teaching, classrooms and community. Indeed our shift is from how students can learn. No longer do we ask "How smart are our kids?" but "How Are Kids Smart?" A must for every classroom teacher struggling with the challenges of increasing diversity, inclusion of students with special needs and the move toward heterogeneous grouping.
A note to Special Educators: Observe a student with disabilities in an M.I. program and the parent's perspective.

Also Available in Español!

Teacher & Administrator Versions

Teacher Version
Price: $69.00
Order: #V-VMIT
VHS, 31 minutes

Administrator Version
Price: $99.00
Order: #V-VKSA
VHS, 41 minutes

Español (Spanish subtitles; Teacher version only): Price: $79.00; Order #VS-VKST

Emotional Intelligence: A New Vision For Educators
Dr. Daniel Goleman

Based on his best selling book, Emotional Intelligence: Why it can matter more than IQ, Daniel Goleman's fascinating and persuasive video argues that our view of human intelligence is far too narrow. Drawing on groundbreaking research, Goleman shows that Emotional Intelligence is more important than IQ. It is a different way of being smart that is more critical to success in life. Research indicates that our emotions play a much greater role in decision making and individual success than has been commonly acknowledged. Given the serious problems of student discipline, violence, teen pregnancy, substance abuse and school dropouts, the role of emotional literacy in education is essential. These problems are symptoms of deficits in Emotional Intelligence. Find out what we can do as educators to effectively incorporate Emotional Intelligence into our classrooms.

Also Available in Español!

Price: $89.95
Order: #V-VEIN
VHS, 38 minutes

Español version (Spanish subtitles): Price: $99.95; Order #VS-VEIS

Title I
Title III

Multiple Intelligences and the Second Language Learner
Presented by Jo Gusman

Jo Gusman, nationally renowned expert on second language learners, presents a compelling argument for the use of multiple intelligences theory in our nation's classrooms. Observe first-hand how innovative programs in California are incorporating multiple intelligences building on students' strengths and abilities. Learn how you can reach and teach the second language learner in creative ways that focus on educational environments that recognize their multiple intelligences.

Also Available in Español!

Price: $99.95
Order: #V-MIS
VHS, 40 minutes

Español version (Spanish subtitles): Price: $109.95; Order #VS-MISSP

Add to your professional library with videos focusing on one of the best methods to differentiate instruction:

Brain-Based Education–Videos

Optimizing Intelligences: Thinking, Emotion & Creativity
Hosted by Peter Salovey; Featuring Howard Gardner, Daniel Goldman, Mihaly Csikszentmihaly, Renilde Montessori, Jo Gusman

Three of the most internationally renowned authorities whose theories and research are transforming our thinking about learning, intelligence and happiness in order to answer the question: How do we develop human potential? Hosted by **Peter Salovey,** co-founder of **emotional intelligence theory,** this video explores three of the most innovative paradigms about **human growth, learning, and potential** from the following psychologists: **Mihaly Csikszentmihalyi,** professor at the University of Chicago and author of the national best seller *Flow;* **Howard Gardner,** author of **Multiple Intelligences;** and **Daniel Goleman,** author of the international best seller *Emotional Intelligence.* Also included are staff from Four Winds Hospital in New York, as well as world renown educators **Renilde Montessori** of the Assoc. Montessori Internationale, **Maurice Elias,** Professor at Rutgers University, and **Jo Gusman,** educational consultant on second language learners.

Also Available in Español!

Title I

Price: $99.95
Order: #V-VOPI
VHS, 45 minutes

Español version (Spanish subtitles): Price: $109.95; Order #VS-VOPS

Rainbows of Intelligence:
Raising Student Performance Through Multiple Intelligences
Dr. Sue Teele

Dr. Sue Teele, author of the book Rainbows of Intelligence: Exploring How Students Learn, uses a powerful metaphor to help us better understand the implementation of multiple intelligences' strategies in the classroom. The viewer will see exciting illustrations that highlight MI as a powerful way of improving instruction and student learning as well as meeting higher standards. Sue Teele is supported by the nationally recognized author and speaker Dr. Thomas Armstrong, as well as staff from Country Springs Elementary School in Chino Hills, CA and other respected educators. In this metaphoric presentation you will learn how educators can redesign the curriculum to enhance every students' ability to learn.

Also Available in Español!

Title I

Price: $99.95
Order: #V-VROI
VHS, 38 minutes

Español version (Spanish subtitles): Price: $109.95; Order #VS-VROISP

Multiple Intelligences: Discovering the Giftedness in All
Presented by: Thomas Armstrong
Featuring Dr. Sue Teele and Jo Gusman

Dr. Thomas Armstrong, one of the most nationally acclaimed lecturers in the area of Multiple Intelligences (MI), presents an array of teaching strategies to discover giftedness in all children. In this video, Dr. Armstrong is joined by other leaders in education - Dr. Sue Teele, Director of Education Extension, University of California, Riverside; Jo Gusman, Educational Consultant; Bruce Campbell, teacher and author of articles and books in the area of MI, and others - who share their views and experiences related to multiple intelligences. Also, presented are numerous school scenes which demonstrate creative teaching strategies that can be implemented. Explore the most current thinking on MI and its application in our nation's classrooms including the 8th intelligence, "the Naturalist". Designed for staff development, this video is for educators who wish to enhance the learning process by identifying the variety of ways in which children can be viewed through their giftedness.

Also Available in Español!

Title I

Price: $79.00
Order: #V-MIDG
VHS, 44 minutes

Español version (Spanish subtitles): Price: $89.00; Order #VS-MIDGSP

Classroom Management

Win-Win Discipline: Strategies for All Discipline Problems
(All Grades)
Spencer Kagan, Patricia Kyle, & Sally Scott

If we end a disruption, we improve our classroom for a while. If instead we foster autonomous responsibility, we prevent future disruptions and empower our students for a lifetime. Win-Win provides proven step-by-step strategies and structures to prevent disruptions, for the moment-of-disruption, and follow-ups. Go beyond manipulative tricks to end disruptions. Use Win-Win's proven approach to prevent disruptions by teaching learned responsibility.

- Turns anger into rational decision-making
- Replaces boredom with active engagement
- Channels excess energy into productive learning
- Ends control-seeking via learned self-efficacy
- Transforms attention seeking into self-validation
- Converts avoidance of failure into self-confidence

With Win-Win, you create a safe, comfortable learning environment for your and your students — A place where students are excited to come and where you don't feel stressed by the end of the day. Win the freedom to focus on learning and growing, not on disruptions.

Price: $39.00
Order: #B-BKWW

NEW!

Title I

Deluxe Classroom Chimes

Creating a positive brain-compatible learning environment for children and adults has always been a top priority for Jo, so much so, that Jo is never without her desk chime at every seminar she presents. Originally a part of her classroom management process, Jo used her chimes to signal transitions, and to get her students' attention.

Price: $31.95
Order: #A-F-CHM

FONTS4TEACHERS CD-ROM AND BOOK

Did you know that there are only 5 main handwriting "families" that dominate our world? These main writing "families" do not coincide with boundaries of language or country, but tend to cover vast zones of civilization. The 5 main writing families are: Chinese, Latin, Indian, Arab, and Cyrillic. This may explain why some of your ELL students learn to write in English, a Latin script system, faster than other ELL students. To help your students master their new handwriting system, Jo Gusman recommends you use the Fonts4Teachers program. These programs will allow you to create tailored handwriting worksheets using the culturally relevant, thematic vocabulary you choose to have your students practice.

Single user license:
Price: $39.95
Order: #S-FFTS
Unlimited school license:
Price: $399.95
Order: #S-FFTU

Single user license:
Price: $24.95
Order: #S-CATS
Unlimited school license:
Price: $249.95
Order: #S-CATU

Single user license:
Price: $39.95
Order: #S-HFTS
Unlimited school license:
Price: $399.95
Order: #S-HFTU

Title I

Title III

Cooperative Learning

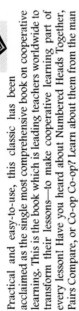

Title I

Cooperative Learning
Dr. Spencer Kagan (All Grades)

Practical and easy-to-use, this classic has been acclaimed as the single most comprehensive book on cooperative learning. This is the book which is leading teachers worldwide to transform their lessons—to make cooperative learning part of every lesson! Have you heard about Numbered Heads Together, Pairs Compare, or Co-op Co-op? Learn about them from the man who created most co-op "structures." Would you like dozens of students' social skills? Or 100's of ready-to-use teambuilding and class building activities to make your class click? This book has it all. You will find easy, step-by-step approaches to teamformation, classroom set-up and management, thinking skills and mastery, lesson planning, scoring and recognition, and research and theory. Tables, graphics, and reproducibles make cooperative learning easy, fun, and successful. 392 pages.

Price: $39.00
Order: #B-BCL

Transparency Cooperative Learning Spinners

Use these convenient classroom management tools to add variety to your classroom! With the **Student** and **Team Spinners**, you will be able to ensure equal opportunity for all to respond, whether during a class project or a classroom responsibility. The **Question Spinner** provides excellent question starters for all types of thinking and is a great way to integrate higher-level thinking across the curriculum.

Price: $8.00 for all 3
Order: #C-TCLS

SmartCards

SmartCards are precisely that—a very *smart card* and extremely useful classroom tool. This quick reference guide provides concise background knowledge about its topic (Cooperative Learning, Multiple Intelligences, Mind Mapping, Graphic Organizers), including tips, key concepts, classroom ideas and loads of activities on each colorful, laminated guide. These SmartCards support classroom curriculum and are excellent guides for teaching organizational tools in the differentiated classroom. An absolute must for every classroom and effective classroom instruction.

Price: $12.00 for all 4
Order: #C-SS

Save 10% by ordering this set

Cooperative Learning Classroom Combo

All items on this page included!

Provide your classroom with:

✦ Cooperative Learning Book
✦ All 3 Transparency Spinners
✦ All 4 Laminated SmartCards

A $55.00 Value, at 10% off!
Price: $49.50
Order: #C-CL

Title I

Bundles to Save You Time &Money!

ELL Teacher Combo

Purchase all three of these books to ensure you will incorporate new and effective strategies in your lessons! Administrators, give this great package to your teachers or provide it in your professional development library at your school. Each book provides a variety of strategies to meet the diverse learning needs of your students!

Price: $89.86
Order: #C-ELLTC

Save 10%!
($99.85 if purchased separately)

Administrator Combo

As an administrator, your concerns cover many areas. Learn the latest research on the brain and standards-based assessment, as well as view examples of lessons using differentiated instruction in Jo Gusman's latest video. Use this package to address the role you play in ensuring that all of yours students' needs are being met, while still providing the leadership role your district demands of you.

DVD: $177.21
Price: $177.21
Order: #C-AC1DVD

VHS: $177.21
Price: $177.21
Order: #C-AC1VHS

Save 10%!
($196.90 if purchased separately)

CALL US TO CUSTOM MAKE YOUR COMBO. HOW CAN WE HELP YOU MEET YOUR

School & Community

Debunking the Middle-Class Myth: Why Diverse Schools Are Good For All Kids
Eileen Gale Kugler

Former journalist and parent Eileen Gale Kugler offers a unique perspective on what every educator, parent, and community leader should know about reaping the rich harvest of our diverse schools. This book provides guidance on how we can all work together to dispel the myths and nurture the opportunities of a school environment with a vibrant mix of races and cultures. Anecdotes from Kugler's personal experience are included as well as information from 80 interviews with key educators, parents, and students.

Price: $23.50
Order: #B-4512

Bridging School and Home Through Family Nights: Ready-to-Use Plans for Grades K-8
Diane W. Kyle, Ellen McIntyre, Karen B. Miller, & Gayle H. Moore

NEW!

Research confirms the link between family involvement and academic success. Yet, as student populations become increasingly diverse, educators face a daunting challenge in establishing close connections with families. Find all the information, materials, and resources for planning and implementing events that build effective relationships. Drawing on their own experiences and extensive research, the authors include information on adapting events for special populations, issues around providing food and incentives, cost-saving ideas, and additional resources.

Each family night chapter provides event procedures, needed materials, connections with national standards, and numerous reproducibles, including invitations, agendas, sign-in sheets, evaluation forms, activity worksheets, handouts, and overheads. Productive family night experiences offer an enjoyable and meaningful way for schools to reach out to families and get them involved. This book is appropriate for K-8 teachers and principals or anyone in the school or district responsible for family events.

Price: $32.95
Order: #B-1467-1

More titles to add humor or direction to staff meetings!

- **If You're Riding a Horse and It Dies, Get Off!**
- **Looking Forward to Monday Morning**
- **If You Don't Feed the Teachers They Eat the Students**

Price: $15.95
Order: #B-457-2

Price: $32.95
Order: #B-300

Price: $7.95
Order: #B-5836

NEW HORIZONS IN EDUCATION, INC.
2443 Fair Oaks Boulevard #365
Sacramento, California 95825-7684

ORDER FORM: PLEASE COMPLETE AND FAX TO : 916-482-4433; OR EMAIL US @: info@nhie.net
HAVE ANY QUESTIONS, PLEASE CONTACT US AT 1-800-573-NHIE (6443)
OR VISIT US AT *www.nhie.net*

SHIP TO:
NAME: _____

GRADE LEVEL/POSITION: _____

SCHOOL/INSTITUTION: _____

STREET ADDRESS: _____

CITY: _____ STATE: _____ ZIP: _____

SCHOOL PHONE: _____ _____

HOME PHONE: _____ _____

EMAIL ADDRESS: _____

BILL TO:
☐ CHECK IF SAME AS SHIPPING ADDRESS

NAME: _____

GRADE LEVEL/POSITION: _____

SCHOOL/INSTITUTION: _____

STREET ADDRESS: _____

CITY: _____ STATE: _____ ZIP: _____

SCHOOL PHONE: _____ _____

HOME PHONE: _____ _____

EMAIL ADDRESS: _____

ITEM #	TITLE/DESCRIPTION	PRICE	QTY.	TOTAL PRICE

CHECK HERE TO RECEIVE A FREE MOTIVATIONAL T-SHIRT WHEN YOUR ORDER EXCEEDS $500.00! ☐

SUBTOTAL:	
CA RESIDENTS ADD SALES TAX:	
SHIPPING & HANDLING CHARGES**	
TOTAL AMOUNT:	

METHOD OF PAYMENT:

☐ Check or Money Order
(made out to New Horizons in Education, Inc.)

☐ Purchase Order (Purchase Orders must be faxed or mailed)

☐ MasterCard ☐ Visa P.O. #:_____

CREDIT CARD #:_____

SIGNATURE:_____ EXPIRATION DATE_____

** FOR ORDERS TOTALING LESS THAN $75.00 ADD $5.00 PER ITEM.

ORDERS TOTALING $75.01 AND ABOVE ADD 10% OF TOTAL AMOUNT DUE, NOT TO EXCEED $85.00.

PLEASE CALL FOR SHIPPING COSTS OUTSIDE THE U.S.

FOR ALL SHIPMENTS OUTSIDE THE U.S AND CANADA, ORDERS MUST BE PREPAID IN U.S. DOLLARS.

NEW HORIZONS IN EDUCATION, INC.
"KEEPERS AND POLISHERS"

1. Describe 3 keepers from today's seminar.

2. List 2 ideas you will implement.

3. List polishers that would help us provide you with a more effective seminar.

4. List a polisher that would help Jo be a better teacher.

We would appreciate any comments you have about today's seminar:

YOUR NAME

ADDRESS ☐ HOME ☐ SCHOOL (CHECK ONE)

CITY   STATE   ZIP CODE

(_____)
PHONE NUMBER

E-MAIL

POSITION   SCHOOL DISTRICT/INSTITUTION

☆ May we use your name and comments in future brochures and web site?

YES   NO

Thank you for your feedback . We look forward to seeing you again!